WHATEVE
"PLEASE" AND "THANK YOU"?

We live in a world where respect, gratitude, and appreciation have been replaced by efficiency, dismissiveness, and even fear of genuine connection. Sometimes, we don't stare up from our screens and devices long enough to realize there is even another person on the other side of the tweet or email. "Is anybody out there?"

One thing is for sure: this speed of life has taken a toll on our basic use of good manners and etiquette. Nowhere is this more apparent than in the decline of professional business communications. But manners and etiquette can be a powerful tool for business and sales success. *It Begins with Please and Doesn't End with Thank You* will show you how to regain those tools and techniques of bygone eras and update them for the digital today.

This how-to guide and go-to resource takes the concepts of "please" and "thank you" into every realm where you engage with clients and prospects—from your first hellos and emails, phone and video calls, to conference rooms and restaurants. With his "return to the personal" philosophy, sales veteran Edwin P. Baldry breaks down the practices, principles, and protocols for successful business dealings and relationship-building. Via tips, tools, and humorous tales, Baldry shows how to tap into the often-overlooked power of manners to improve your business relationships, and how to transfer etiquette into sales performance.

IT BEGINS WITH

PLEASE

AND DOESN'T END WITH

THANK YOU

IT BEGINS WITH
PLEASE
AND DOESN'T END WITH
THANK
YOU

TRANSFORMING BUSINESS ETIQUETTE
INTO SALES PERFORMANCE

EDWIN P. BALDRY

RIVER GROVE
BOOKS

Published by River Grove Books
Austin, TX
www.rivergrovebooks.com

Distributed by River Grove Books

Design and composition by The Book Designers
Cover design by The Book Designers
Front cover images © Shutterstock

Publisher's Cataloging-in-Publication data is available.

Print ISBN: 978-1-63299-459-2

eBook ISBN: 978-1-63299-460-8

First Edition

For Momski

"Everyone you meet is fighting a battle you
know nothing about. Be kind. Always."
—ROBIN WILLIAMS

"Hit every door there is, bang it as hard as you can.
Every now and then, one will open, but most of them don't.
The next year you go back and you bang those doors again."
—DR. SHIRLEY WEBER

"Be courteous, kind, and genuine all the time.
You'll have a much better chance of getting that back in return."
—JEFF "JJ" JELLISON

"Be fortunate enough to have cool clients."
—TOM NEWTON

"Don't ever think there is nothing to learn about yourself
and the people around you. Every event, every person,
every situation we encounter is a teacher."
—JOSEPH DEITCH

CONTENTS

FOREWORD

I am honored to introduce you to Edwin P. Baldry. If you're in the corporate, treasury, or institutional finance industries, you probably know Ed. If you're in institutional finance and haven't met him, then you're probably doing jail time.

In 2010, I was introduced to the Institutional Cash Distributors (ICD) founding partners: Tom Newton, Jeff Jellison, and Ed Baldry. These three were an extraordinary triumvirate of sales talent, pursuing a mission to transform institutional investment trading with an independent web-based liquidity portal for global corporate treasuries. I came on board as the CMO. It was an amazing run.

Having worked in Los Angeles and Hollywood for decades, I thought I had already seen everything. I'd had a notable career working for international hotelier Barron Hilton; legendary film director Steven Spielberg; music icons Ray Charles, Tony Bennett, Toto's Steve Lukather, Clint Black, and Tina Turner; and insurance industry titan Stanley Beyer. All were incredible, inspiring business and creative personalities.

But Baldry, Jellison, and Newton were uniquely different. They were onto something bigger and more ambitious. Baldry, Co-CEO, guided ICD's global sales force and launched ICD's London sales and trading operations. Thanks to his high-profile presence across the US and international markets, enterprise-level treasuries, asset managers, fund companies, and industry specialists all took notice.

In my formative years I led a marketing agency, WorldWest Communications. I was introduced to the classic "go-to" writing guide, *The Elements of Style* by William Strunk and E. B. White. It quickly became my everyday English-language resource—the kind of book that becomes dog-eared from use. It didn't tell you what to write but how to write it better. The same is true with Baldry's *It Begins with Please and Doesn't End with Thank You: Transforming Business Etiquette into Sales Performance*. His book is an evergreen, everyday manners and etiquette resource that is rich in content, clearly explained, and joyfully written. It can make you both a better salesperson and a better person.

It Begins with Please and Doesn't End with Thank You is a treasure chest of principles, protocols, and processes of collective wisdom, beautifully laid out and organized for easy consumption—and re-consumption. Ed makes solid sense of the many mysteries that lead to success in sales. Whether your mission is selling widgets or managing highly complex, consultative sales, the processes are the same, the protocols are unchanging, and, when properly practiced, the long-term results are often amazing.

The book's Preface begins: "Somehow, somewhere along the way, civilization has become quite uncivilized." With the specter of social media dumbing down our everyday connections and conversations, and with the rapid disappearance of face-to-face meetings due to the global pandemic, manners and traditional etiquette have largely disappeared from public life. This is Ed's fundamental battleground and the fulcrum that he pivots on to teach, illuminate, and illustrate the ageless values of business etiquette and manners.

Ed owns etiquette. In his business world, he is the standard-bearer of manners. He gets up from his chair when a lady approaches the table. He ushers everyone else through the door first. He always offers to pay when the bill comes. His touch is nuanced but holds depth, demonstrating the profound power of his politeness and gratitude. The sincerity of his efforts and the warmth of his enthusiasm are real—not merely techniques—and they are always turned on. Whether on stage, in a boardroom, in front of an industry audience, at the dinner table, or riding shotgun in a car, Baldry brings his exquisite manners everywhere.

There is another invaluable quality that accompanies his manners: Ed has the "gift of funny." This is his calling card. It is part of who he is, and its effect is palpable. Anyone who has ever spent time with him, in business or in play, knows this. Ed exudes a sanguine, insatiable, high-energy sense of humor that is inarguably transmissible.

Yet perhaps Ed's greatest skill-set lies in teaching, coaching, and mentoring—sharing what he's learned from the thousands of sales presentations he's made. Ed teaches what works and what doesn't, and what it takes to improve your sales acuity and professional IQ.

There is plenty of amazing stuff in this book. Dig in. Read it from beginning to end, and then from end to beginning. Apply and integrate these lessons into your sales repertoire. For the interested reader, an education begins with reading this book, and it doesn't end with having read it.

—Doug Brown, Co-Founder and CMO, Wellness Responder

INTRODUCTION

"Life is short, but there is always time enough for courtesy."
—**RALPH WALDO EMERSON**

"It begins with please and doesn't end with thank you." This concept might seem like a strange play on words. But hang on as I go out on a limb—or as we both go out on a limb together. These words encapsulate the premise of this book.

"Please" and "thank you" form the DNA of our understanding of politeness. In other words, they epitomize good manners—all of society's commonly accepted behaviors, our prevailing customs and habits, and every social grace you bestow upon others.

As my mother, Anne Baldry, used to say: "Manners are an opportunity to show anyone respect, without a need for reciprocity." Her words have stuck with me. What my mom meant was this: we offer our good manners to friends, family, associates, and strangers not because we have to or expect them to be returned in kind, but because these gestures are the right thing to do.

Like it or not, manners are part of the social contract. And that includes the business environment.

But here's the thing. Somehow, somewhere along the way, civilization has become quite uncivilized—to our detriment. We've lost something that took centuries to develop, refine, and perfect, namely manners and etiquette. In today's business environment, this lack of attention to manners has left us sometimes ill-equipped or floundering. We struggle through meetings, conversations, and connections that are too often, and sometimes shockingly, short on basic social graces.

Most people *do* know about etiquette, and most of the time (unless they're jerks) people don't intend to disrespect each other. But the absence of rudeness does not equal courtesy. Thanks to technology and modern communication, we have endless ways to connect, if only fleetingly, but we often don't converse. In particular, generations of digital natives are becoming less comfortable with face-to-face conversations, preferring to text, Snapchat, and TikTok.

Reviving the art of etiquette in the 21st century doesn't mean reviving outdated ideas. I'm not proposing that lords lay cloaks over rain puddles and urge the safe passage of their womenfolk with a bow and a "M'lady." How we behave in a business context must be responsive to and respectful of current social events and movements, both in this country and around the world; such movements are constantly reshaping acceptable ways to interact with others. Etiquette also needs to adapt to the challenges of the coronavirus and other potential pandemics down the road.

But all of these new developments—medical, digital, societal—provide opportunities to revisit the core practices, principles, and protocols of business and sales, and how good manners pertain to them. This book will ponder these questions.

Transforming Business Etiquette into Sales Performance

"Times like these always reveal that the veil of civility
is thinner than we thought...but that the hearts of
good people are greater than we imagined."
—STEVE MARABOLI

In essence, "please" has always been the starting gun of polite and professional communications. But it's important to note that "thank you" does not represent a limit or an end to those communications. We must go beyond these niceties.

In this book, I want to take the concepts of manners and etiquette—"please" and "thank you"—even further. Together, we'll examine every realm where you engage with customers and prospects: from your first hellos and phone calls, through emails and video calls, to conference halls and dining rooms—anywhere you interact with your business clients.

By manners and etiquette, I mean an ethos of respect, gratitude, and appreciation that should permeate the entire experience, for both the salesperson and the customer. When these qualities are present in every step of your business communications and sales process, and are genuinely expressed and apparent to all involved, then good things begin to happen. They can jumpstart relationships with clients that last for years, even decades.

In short, manners and etiquette are powerful tools for business. In this book we'll discuss how thoughtful attention to respect, gratitude, and appreciation can result in:

- Improved productivity
- More frequent and more meaningful communications with your clients and prospects
- Stronger, even lifelong, relationships with your clients and prospects
- Bigger and better (and longer-tenured) clients
- Better, stronger, and more profitable businesses
- And other positive outcomes in your personal and professional life

I am a career sales professional. As an early participant in the financial technology sector, I was a co-founding partner of a global investment and risk-management company, Institutional Cash Distributors (ICD). Our company worked with some of the biggest players on the planet, including global enterprise companies across multiple sectors, such as Apple, Coca-Cola, Facebook, Google, Home Depot, and McDonald's. I've spent over thirty years either selling or managing salespeople all over the country and the world. And if I've learned anything in all my mentoring of sales teams, it's this: most "coachable and teachable moments" in sales come down to the proper application of manners and etiquette.

What's more, leveraging proper sales etiquette and simple good manners—what I call the "please" and "thank you" principle—can play a transformational role in your professional and personal lives.

How to Get the Most Out of This Book

"I have never met a man so ignorant that
I couldn't learn something from him."
—GALILEO GALILEI

It Begins with Please and Doesn't End with Thank You is divided into four parts:

• **Part 1: FACE the Day:** This section provides general advice to get you, as a salesperson, into the best possible shape to prepare you for success.

• **Part 2: Preparation:** This section offers techniques for the early stages of your business relationships, including greetings, due diligence, and establishing rapport.

• **Part 3: Performance:** This section lays out techniques for the middle stages of your dealings—maintaining relationships, presentation skills, the transfer of enthusiasm, and active listening.

• **Part 4: Modes of Communication:** This final section provides suggestions for the use of phone, email, social media, meals, entertainment and events, and handwritten notes.

There's also an **Appendix**, offering a planning guide for business, sales, and industry events.

Each chapter examines both old and new principles of business etiquette. Beyond mothers and manners, mentors and managers, we're going to break down several principles, strategies, and secrets to successful sales and relationship-building. It's not just talk; there's also technique. You'll learn how to put these ideas into practice.

Throughout the book, we'll explore examples of my own sales experiences and business relationships that have influenced my life and career. To that end, you'll hear plenty of personal anecdotes about my encounters with dozens of outstanding business people who have helped to shape my incredibly fortunate run in sales.

Most chapters contain the following elements:

• **EDibles:** Personal stories from the trenches, and examples drawn from my own life and business career. ("EDibles"…what was I thinking?)

• **The Core Principle:** A clear description of an etiquette principle, with an explanation of why it's important in a sales and business setting.

• **Putting the Principle into Play:** Detailed instructions and suggestions for how to put a principle into practice. Sometimes this includes lists of "Dos" and "Don'ts," which I call **"Try This"** and **"Don't Try This."**

• **Pandemic Protocols:** Recommendations for how to adapt manners and etiquette in light of the coronavirus and other new forces in the digital and social realms.

• Powerful, inspirational, and thought-provoking quotes.

The advice in these pages pertains to sales and business relationships. In sharing with you my vision for what good manners and etiquette in today's business climate can look like, I'll keep what's worked before, adapt what makes sense, chuck what doesn't, and propose new ideas to roll with the changes. Some of you may find that this advice applies to other aspects of your life as well, and you may even find parts that are personally transformational. (Note: while I'm sometimes a clever guy, I'm not a therapist.) Some of these protocols and techniques you'll like immediately. Some you might choose to leave behind. Figure out what works for you.

Am I going to make a big promise about what this book will do for you? No. Do I have all the answers? No. But I believe this book will help you gain a better grasp of how to boost your business success, based on the foundation of manners and etiquette, respect, gratitude, and appreciation. If you assimilate even one tool, borrow one trick of the trade, or perfect one technique from these pages, and that helps you win even one more deal, reading this book will be well worth your time, and mine.

I appreciate your time and consideration. I hope you find these principles as rewarding and helpful to your career as they've been to mine. Let's get to work. The starting gun of "please" and "thank you" has just fired.

All the best!

—EPB
Delray Beach, Florida
September 2020

A Brief History of "Please" and "Thank You"

"Appreciation can change a day, even change a life. Your willingness to put it into words is all that is necessary."—**Margaret Cousins**

We're all familiar with the concepts of "please" and "thank you." Or, at least, we all should be. Any polite request or transaction, whether with confidantes or with strangers, typically begins with a "please" and ends with a "thank you." In line at the grocery store, chatting with a bank teller, asking for bread from a server at a restaurant, receiving helpful information on the phone from a customer-service agent, making room for a fellow traveler in a packed commuter train—in everyday social situations such as these, unless you've been raised by wolves or trolls, the words "please" and "thank you" come almost automatically, even if you'll probably never cross paths with those people again.

From childhood onward, both preaching and practice constantly remind us that these "magic words" increase our likelihood of getting what we want. Whether the request is for a service or for someone's time or assistance, "please" has always been the key to the city. After receiving the service or assistance, "thank you" has always been a polite and impactful way to express gratitude to the person who has helped you.

David Graeber's book *Debt: The First 5,000 Years* discusses the lesser-known origins of the use of "please" and "thank you":

• **In English, "please" is shorthand for "if you please" and "if it pleases you to do this."**

• **The root of the phrase "thank you" comes from "think," e.g., "I will think about what you did for me."**

• In some languages, "thank you" translates as "much obliged" or "I am in your debt." In French, "merci" (thank you) means to beg for mercy.

• The replies "You're welcome," "My pleasure," or "No problem" are all ways of saying, "You're off the hook, you're not in my debt."

• The widespread use of "please" and "thank you" emerged in the 16th and 17th centuries, as the middle classes began to work in offices and shop in stores.

Graeber goes on to say that over the course of the last five hundred years, as business practices spread, so did the use of "please" and "thank you." As he puts it, these polite terms have become part of "a much larger philosophy, a set of assumptions of what humans are and what they owe one another, that have by now become so deeply ingrained that we cannot see them."

It Begins with Please and Doesn't End with Thank You explores the impact of applying this "much larger philosophy" and this "set of assumptions" to sales and business practices. The "please" and "thank you" principle can help to deliver success and the happiness that successful outcomes can bring you.

1

F.A.C.E. THE DAY

CHAPTER 1

F.A.C.E. THE DAY

EDibles: Only from the Mind of Minolta

"You are only young once, and if you work it right, once is enough."
—JOE E. LEWIS

In 1991, I was twenty-two and fresh out of college. I had just spent two weeks on the beach after graduating from San Diego State University, having majored in Speech Communications with a minor in Philosophy. By June, I had blown through most of my graduation gift money. It was time to move on from being one of the guys still partying and sleeping on one couch, then another. It was time to give up my dream of a stand-up comedy career, which I had taken seriously in college but now realized was not going to make me any money. It was time to leave town and begin a new life called "adulthood."

I arrived in San Francisco a few days later, my '82 Jetta loaded to the gills with all my worldly possessions: shorts, t-shirts, a Mexican blanket, a San Diego State beer mug, and my two new graduation gifts: two business suits, one blue, one gray. In a lucky break, I got my start in "copier sales," known at the time to be one of the toughest proving grounds for entry-level sales personnel. During the early 1990s, copier companies would pretty much hire anybody with a college degree, a pulse, and a smile. The jobs were all straight commission gigs, so the copier companies at the time—Canon, Xerox, Lanier, Toshiba, Minolta—had little to lose by hiring beginners.

Chuck Maguire, the regional manager for Minolta Business Systems in the Bay Area, called me in for an interview. That day, dressed in my new blue suit, a red tie, and a freshly pressed white shirt (the "Jack Welch uniform," may he rest in peace), I rode shotgun on a "field ride" with one of Chuck's top sales guys, his nephew, Chris Spingola. The purpose of a field ride is to see if interested candidates have both the stomach and the discipline for the gig. Chris was spectacular. I loved the way he walked, talked, and operated. He moved with confidence, spoke with purpose and a smile. This guy was smooth. I wanted not only to be that guy but to beat that guy. In short, I was hooked. When we got back to the office, Chuck asked what I thought and I simply said, "I love it. I could kill at this job." Already I had fallen in love with sales.

I was young. I was eager. But as a sales guy still wet behind the ears, I was also looking for guidance. I needed a mantra. And while I was working for Minolta, I found one: **F.A.C.E. the Day.**

F.A.C.E. the Day: The Core Principle

"You can't take over the world without a good acronym."
—C. S. WOOLLEY

In professional sales, we love acronyms and mantras that help us improve our skills and ultimately our performance. If you've ever been part of a team or trained relentlessly for any skill, you've seen or utilized mantras.

Originally, in the Hindu and Buddhist traditions, a mantra came from the Vedas, a body of Sanskrit religious texts originating in ancient India. A mantra was a sacred utterance—a syllable, word, or group of words believed to have religious, magical, or spiritual powers. It was also a word or sound that could be repeated to aid concentration in meditation. Nowadays mantras are more mundane. They are frequently repeated statements, slogans, formulas, or truisms. Sometimes mantras are merely clichés: "Life's not fair," "You get what you pay for," "K.I.S.S.—Keep It Simple, Stupid."

"Mantras…help you focus on what you want to create for that day."
—KAROL WARD

The more original and clever mantras can serve as affirmations, ways to motivate and inspire yourself, your team, or your company. Here are a few such mantras (or acronyms that are mantras), taken from personal, business, and sports contexts. Some you might recognize, others perhaps not:

• **"Play like a champion today." (Team slogan, University of Notre Dame Fighting Irish football program)**

• **"Just win, baby." (Al Davis, general manager of the Oakland Raiders)**

• **"Don't let anyone work harder than you do." (Serena Williams)**

• **"Victory requires payment in advance." (Anonymous)**

• **"Clear eyes, full hearts, can't lose" (Team slogan, from the TV show *Friday Night Lights*)**

• **"The will to win is not nearly so important as the will to prepare to win." (Vince Lombardi)**

• **"T.E.A.M.—Together Excellence, Alone Mediocrity" (Anonymous)**

• **"The harder you work, the luckier you get." (Pro golfer Gary Player)**

Throughout this book, I'll be quoting and referencing some of the best salespeople, business icons, and inspirational humans. As in the stand-up comedy business, "borrowing," or repurposing good content in business writing, is not punishable by death.

As I mentioned, I was at Minolta when I discovered my first mantra, F.A.C.E. the Day, or F.A.C.E. for short. As it turns out... *ta-da!*...this mantra is *also* an acronym. It stands for:

FOCUS

ATTITUDE

CONTROL

EMPATHY

Early in my career, I began to use this magic mantra in my own work. Initially I borrowed parts and principles of F.A.C.E. from the marvelous Paul Warshaw (R.I.P.), another regional manager in Los Angeles for Minolta, as well as from the unbeatable Jim Graff, who was in a class by himself in our San Francisco sales office. Over the years, I've continued to adapt and hone and perfect the four basic principles of F.A.C.E.

Before we unleash your inner sales beast into the battlefield of business, and before we harness all the superpowers of manners or etiquette, we need to prepare you for success. We need you to zero in on you. That's why in this section I break down and discuss the impact of each component of the mantra—**FOCUS, AT**TITUDE, **C**ONTROL, and **EM**PATHY—and explain how you can apply them to your own life.

For some of you, the precepts of F.A.C.E. the Day may seem hokey. Trust me, I get it. But I hope that, for most of you, these principles will resonate immediately. Throughout my business career, F.A.C.E. has been a frequent touchstone, a rallying cry, and a blueprint for success. Now I want to pass it onto you.

CHAPTER 2

F.A.C.E. THE DAY: FOCUS

EDibles: A Focused Person Is Hard to Beat

"I don't care how much power, brilliance, or energy you have, if you don't harness it and focus it on a specific target, and hold it there, you're never going to accomplish as much as your ability warrants."

—ZIG ZIGLAR

Quite simply, a focused person is hard to beat or deny.

Let me tell you a story about how I used the power of focus to overcome an early and humiliating setback in my formative years.

When I was a teenager growing up in California, I used to race BMX bikes. I was a competitive kid, and I got to be good enough that I made the team sponsored by a local bike shop. My team and I would go to competitions, the shop would pay our entrance fees, and we'd race. That was fun, and we did pretty well. Then, when I was fifteen years old, with a driver's permit but no driver's license, I took my big sister Phyllis's beloved '66 GT Mustang out for a ride on Saint Patrick's Day. I proceeded to wrap her car around a telephone pole, banging up the car to the tune of over a thousand dollars' worth of damage. To repay the repair cost, I needed to earn a thousand bucks. I needed a job, and fast.

Fortunately I had a place in mind. I went back to the bike shop the following day and said, "I need to start working." Before long,

I was working a day or two after school during the week and full-time on the weekends, for a total of twenty hours a week. If my memory serves me, I made minimum wage: $3.25 an hour. After working two weeks, I'd have a check, after taxes, for something like $90.

But that bike-shop gig was critical to me for other reasons than just earning cash. I ended up doing everything in that shop. I dealt with people all day. I learned every inch of the business, from wrenching bikes in the back, to fixing and selling bikes up front, to putting the day's take in the safe each night. I got to the point where, probably by my junior year, after working there for a year and a half, I was managing the bike shop by myself on the weekends. At the time I thought, "Man, do I have it good. I'm managing a bike shop. How cool is that?" Little did I know that I was, essentially, low-priced child labor. I ran the man's entire business for about $24 a day.

But aside from being financially exploited, it was a great experience. I had no supervision. I had the responsibility of always having to show up to open the shop (no matter how hungover I was). Hard work equals freedom, and that definitely paid dividends, because that freedom earned me more freedom, allowing me to grow and gradually acquire more and more responsibility. For me, the lesson resonates to this day: the harder you work, the more freedom you get (and the more you'll get left alone by your boss).

Also, at $90 a week, I could pay back my sister.

How does this relate to F.A.C.E. the Day? In my case, FOCUS came down to identifying my goals—earn money or suffer the eternal wrath of Phyllis. What should a professional salesperson focus on? Hopefully on many things, but let's begin with focusing on goals. This concept sounds rudimentary: the path to becoming a focused person begins with setting concrete, obtainable goals. But while this concept is talked about a lot, it's surprisingly rarely used.

For the purposes of this book, when I use the term **FOCUS**, I mean focusing on goals in particular.

I believe there are two types of people in the world:

Person 1: "I have a GOAL, and I'm committed to paying the price and working hard to achieve it."

Person 2: "I have a WISH, and my plan is to rub a lamp or buy a lottery ticket to get what I want."

We all know people like Person 2, people with lofty but usually unobtainable wishes: "I want to have a shiny red Ferrari...and only then will I be satisfied and feel good about myself." No harm in dreaming, but Person 2 has forged no viable path for earning or obtaining that shiny red Ferrari. They just know they want it and hope it will appear magically out of thin air.

Person 1 has a concrete goal: "Not only do I want a red Ferrari, but here's how I'm going to get one." Person 1 makes a plan. Person 1 executes that plan, step by step.

In this book, I'll be talking about the kind of people who are committed to earning their goals.

F.A.C.E. the Day: Focus:
Putting the Principle into Play

"The secret to getting started is breaking your complex, overwhelming tasks into small manageable tasks and then starting on the first one."
—MARK TWAIN

Goals are those things that we hold out in front of ourselves, like carrots on sticks, so that we're motivated to develop and commit to a plan to achieve them. In my experience, the trick to achieving them requires more than focus alone. As Twain advises, you also have to break your goals down step by step. Once you've carved them into bite-size portions, these smaller goals will feel attainable and you'll have a better chance of progressing and gaining the needed momentum toward your larger, macro-level goals. That's why I'm going to describe how to reduce your goals down to the ridiculous—*reductio ad absurdum* (that's Latin for "reduction to absurdity").

For the purposes of this discussion, I'll focus on sales and financial-independence goals, not artistic ones. But it goes without saying that there are many other types of goals, including:

• Personal/aspirational goals

• Well-being/health goals

• Familial goals

• Faith goals

• Monetary goals

• Career or professional goals

• Financial goals

Think about one of your own personal goals—perhaps it's to increase the level of joy or satisfaction or love in your life. Your professional or monetary goal might be to obtain a promotion or title, achieve a certain social standing among your peers, earn an award, or make a certain amount of money. A familial goal might be to spend more time with your spouse, and a well-being goal might be to reduce stress or improve your mental or physical health. Goals can be oriented on mindsets and behaviors or on material possessions and other quantifiable things.

When planning for goals, consider that they often play off each other. Reaching a short-term job goal might lead to the achievement of a long-term financial-independence or personal-happiness goal. You might need to quit a draining job or a dead-in-the-water relationship in order to improve your mental health. Some goals are subsets of each other or rely on each other, so it's always a good idea to consider your personal and professional goals holistically.

One should also be able to identify and reverse-engineer for a number of different goals. This process requires some internal analysis and presence of mind—projecting where you'd like to be in five years, ten years, twenty years. You might start by asking, "Where would I like to be personally?" Your answer might be "I'd like to be a happy person," and for you "happy" might mean "I've got a good job, I've got a healthy, happy family, and I have good relationships with my friends." Reflecting on personal goals might lead you to recognize professional ones. Seeing this, you can then effectively reverse-engineer your goals.

Self-reflection about micro and macro goals, as well as weighing "what I want for the future" versus "what is realistic now," can be instrumental in achieving your goals. You might say, "This is not a goal I can work on today, but it's something I can shoot for in five years." Or you might say, "I want to sell this number of Minolta copiers in the Bay Area this year, but my ultimate, macro goal is to build my résumé for the next level of sales job that might have a salary and expense account."

A brainstorming focus exercise such as putting your goals in writing can be helpful. A 2015 study showed that when you write down your goals, you are 33 percent more likely to achieve them, compared with trying to keep them all straight in your head. Make a big list of the top 10 or even top 100 things you want to achieve in life. Divide them into micro and macro goals. Then say, "Okay, achieving everything on this list is not going to be realistic. I need to pick a few to work on now and a few to put in the 'later' column." Learn to prioritize.

Also, motivation can drive goals. Consider what motivates *you*. Accolades, titles, and social standing motivate some of my colleagues. You might be concerned about how you're perceived, while I might be motivated purely by money. Some people don't care if you call them the Whore of Babylon, as long as they're making a million dollars a year. These are all different animals. Managers manage them differently and reward them differently—and you can manage and reward yourself differently too.

Example 1: Focusing on Financial Independence. For the purpose of this discussion, let's consider a macro goal of "financial independence." I'll show you how we can reduce that seemingly monstrous, scary goal down to the ridiculous.

In my experience, financial independence is a fairly common goal. I don't think many people would say, "That isn't something I aspire to." Financial independence doesn't necessarily mean being filthy rich or a dirty rotten scoundrel. It can mean simply supporting yourself at a very modest level.

First, instead of pining for vague dreams of wealth, let's break down and define exactly what "financial independence" means:

• All existing bills and debts paid

• A cushion in the bank of $10K

• The ability to purchase reasonable items without incurring massive debt

By reducing these goals to bite-size portions—a.k.a. "the ridiculous"— we've made achieving them seem more realistic and tangible.

You might ask yourself next, "Okay, smarty-pants, so how can I achieve these goals?" Some options:

- Earn more income

- Spend less

- Shop smarter

Where do we start? Let's take the goal of saving $10,000 by year's end and reverse-engineer it. Hold tight and put on your crash helmets: we're going to use some math. Stashing $10K in the bank by the end of the year breaks down like this:

- $10K divided by 12 months = $833 a month in required savings

- $833 divided by 20 business days = roughly $41 per day

- $41 divided by 8 hours = approximately $5.12 an hour in additional income

See, that didn't hurt your head, did it? In the end, the goal seems easy-peasy. It's very possible to earn an additional $5 an hour or else spend $5 less an hour. In this case, most likely, it will be a combination of both.

By reducing the daunting number of $10K down to a bite-size five bucks an hour, you can make a commitment and take the first step toward your bigger goal. All you need to do is pay a manageable price.

> "The greater danger for most of us lies not in setting
> our aim too high and falling short, but in setting our
> aim too low and achieving our mark."
> **—MICHELANGELO**

Example 2: Focusing on Sales Goals. Let's try another example: a model based on a more ambitious goal with a few more moving parts.

In almost every sales field, cold-calling is a critical part of success. Cold-calling can mean different things depending on your industry—email messages, direct marketing mailings, actual phone calls or knocking on actual doors, and so forth. For this example, let's say the preferred method of your cold-calling routine is sending out an intro packet about your goods or services to your prospects.

What determines the success of your cold-calling? Your conversion ratio.

An early part of any professional sales apprenticeship includes coming to grips with and understanding conversion ratios. In other words, how many cold calls do I need to make to get a qualified lead and, ultimately, a sale? As careers and acumen progress, that conversion ratio goes down for most salespeople. For example, a brand-new rep with zero experience may need to talk to 100 prospects to get a sale, or in this case send out 100 intro packets. A more seasoned, experienced rep might need to reach only 50 prospects to get a win. Keep in mind, any conversion ratio will evolve and change. Therefore, the math on your goals will need to be an ongoing calculation.

Back to our model. Let's say you work in the field of financial product sales or, in my case, during most of my years as a salesman, in institutional money-market funds sales. Often I'd have an annual goal, or quota, for new clients. One year I had a quota of signing 48 new clients. I had arrived at the initial conclusion that my conversion ratio was 25 to 1—for every 25 intro packets I sent out, I'd land one client. In order to achieve my goal of 48 new clients for the year, I would need to send out a certain number of intro packets per year, which meant a certain number per month, per week, and per day. How did I calculate what I needed to do to reach my sales goal in doable, bite-sized chunks? Let's break those numbers down:

• Initial conversion ratio: 25 intro packets = 1 client

• 48 clients = 1,200 intro packets in a year

• 1,200 intro packets in a year = 100 intro packets a month

• 100 intro packets a month = 25 intro packets a week

• 25 intro packets a week = 5 intro packets a day

I knew that 1,200 packets would get me to my 48 clients in a year, and 1,200 seemed overwhelming. But five a day was doable. Figuring out your conversion ratios for cold calls to clients, meetings to clients, and demos to clients are all critical steps in becoming a true sales professional.

Now let's say your next goal is to improve your conversion ratio over the years. This can be done in several different ways, including:

• Better-quality prospecting

• Improved communication and messaging

• An actual groundbreaking product development

• Developing a "sense of smell" for what is really a deal (or not)

• Good old-fashioned experience

As with conversion ratios, you can develop a step-by-step plan to reduce any of these macro goals to the ridiculous.

All this said, when it comes to goals, by which I mean the FOCUS principle in F.A.C.E. the Day, we don't want to short-change ourselves while coming up with these macro goals. That's what our friend Michelangelo was talking about when he warned against "setting our aim too low." This was a guy who took four years, from 1508 to 1512, to paint the Sistine Chapel ceiling. He aimed pretty high. Goal: paint a knockout picture for the Pope's house. No pressure!

My guess is that, to F.A.C.E. his day, he simply reduced each step to the ridiculous: "Okay, Mick. Today, just God's fingertip. Tomorrow, his first knuckle..." Had he set the lofty goal of creating a series of frescoes that would become one of the most intricate, jaw-dropping works of art of all time, he probably never would have made it out of bed each morning.

CHAPTER 3

F.A.C.E. THE DAY: ATTITUDE

EDibles: ICD Was Born from an Opportunity to Work for the Customer

"Weakness of attitude becomes weakness of character."
—ALBERT EINSTEIN

Here's a story that proves how a positive attitude can help you harness your dreams.

Tom Newton, Jeff "JJ" Jellison, and I were fraternity brothers at San Diego State. Since the early 1980s, our lives have intersected in various ways at some of the nation's biggest financial firms: Concord Financial, Scudder Investments, Deutsche Bank, and others. In 2003, for a number of reasons, it was time for the three of us to leave Deutsche Bank and JP Morgan respectively. We wondered, "What if we started our own business?" Tom, JJ, and I put our heads together to discuss the possibility of starting our own fund distribution company.

The writing was clearly on the wall. Our biggest clients were usually using multiple funds—in some cases five, ten, or even twenty or more funds. What if we could provide our clients with all of those funds in one online place, and actually work for the clients instead of representing just one of the names on that list? Institutional money-market funds were basically commoditized at that time. We developed a distribution model that provided all of the industry's biggest funds in one place and did not cost the customer anything for that convenience.

ICD was born.

The product, concept, and solution were all solid. We just needed a few first movers. Tom, JJ, and I each approached our oldest and biggest clients and proposed our "what if." I still vividly remember being enthusiastic about proposing our new model because it was truly client-driven. I was excited about our game plan and positive that it would work. In short, I had a great attitude.

Here's why. Our new money-market fund portal service would be:

• At no cost to the customer

• One application, one wire, and one statement (the "Power of One"), which provided massive efficiencies

• Provided without any long-term contract. If a client was unhappy, they could fire us with a phone call.

My first prospect was Tyco, a large client using multiple funds and running lots of cash. I practically burst into their offices with our new model. I explained its virtues and asked for a shot at all their business. Functionally they had nothing to lose, and they stood to gain both efficiency and cost savings. Throughout my presentation, my positive attitude shone through. I went into the meeting with a great solution that I knew my client would benefit from.

Tyco gave me the nod and soon became one of our first clients. ICD went on to significantly improve their operation.

The moral of this story is that a positive attitude and approach will help you succeed. My belief in our product and our team was real and palpable. Tom, JJ, and I worked together for sixteen more years at ICD. I brought in over twenty different clients that were in some way related to that original Tyco account—now affectionately known as the "Tyco Tree." *Thank you* to our early adopters.

F.A.C.E. the Day: Attitude: Putting the Principle into Play

"Keep your thoughts positive because your thoughts become your words. Keep your words positive because your words become your behavior. Keep your behavior positive because your behavior becomes your habits. Keep your habits positive because your habits become your values. Keep your values positive because your values become your destiny."

—MAHATMA GANDHI

We've all heard axioms about attitude and its impact on outcomes. My personal favorite is "Your attitude determines your altitude." Attitude is the second component of F.A.C.E. the Day.

Here's an analogy I've used when managing salespeople over the years. Imagine a person walking into a crowded bar. The energy of that person usually impacts how they are perceived and received. For example, if some good-looking, well-dressed guy or gal walks in with a smile on their face and a spring in their step, engaging enthusiastically with friends or even strangers, what impression do they make? Most likely, this person is going to be perceived as an attractive, fun, interesting person to hang out with for the evening. And that's going to change their experience, as well as the experiences of those around them.

Conversely, imagine a different person walking into a crowded bar. This person is a poorly dressed grump who sits in a corner all night, moping. Who wants to be part of that sad pity party? No one.

Sales and business relationships work on the same principle. Your attitude can permeate and impact your sales. Here are a few tips and tactics that have proven successful for me and for people I've had the pleasure to work with over the years:

• **Expect Good Things and Engage in Positive Thinking.** Our hopes and emotions can be self-fulfilling prophecies. Assume good outcomes, and they are more likely to happen. Visualization techniques can be helpful as well. Envision the perfect sales call and use that as a mental road-map. Don't let your inner critic tell you, "I'm going to blow it." Those pesky scientists have proven that positive self-talk can make a difference in how you perform.

• **Take Pride in Your Appearance.** This can help you mentally "put on the armor" for an important meeting or call, or jump over any first-impressions hurdle you might encounter. Sometimes, even if I know a conversation will happen over the phone, I'll dress up, shave, and wear shoes instead of my customary flip-flops, in order to feel professional and powerful.

• **Radiate Positivity.** People are drawn to and want to be around positive energy. Try to generate a positive vibe for yourself, so that you're radiating excitement about your business contacts, your company, and your product. (This is a concept we'll explore more thoroughly in **Chapter 11: Transfer of Enthusiasm**.)

Jumping enthusiastically into the breach or attacking the beach with vigor will help you get the numbers you need to achieve your goals. Embracing your targets and acknowledging them is a crucial part of a positive outlook, and doing so will make them become less daunting and more promising. "I know what's on the other side of those hundred cold calls: successful outcomes!"

Here's where a mantra can help. One of the most successful daily mantras that I used at Minolta was "Today is a great day to sell copiers." This is a play on the slightly more serious "Today is a good day to die," frequently attributed to the Oglala Lakota Indian war-leader Crazy Horse. Yes, my cheeky mantra was mocked at first, but I stuck with it. Before long, the catchphrase took off and was adopted by several other reps and managers. It became a battle cry for most of the San Francisco office as we went out into the field for the day, the perfect salvo for 22-year-olds passing each other in the halls and heading into the cold-calling abyss. "Today is a great day to sell copiers" was a funny, harmless, and positive way to adjust our attitudes, feel a sense of camaraderie, and begin the day on an upbeat note.

Here are a few other valuable tips for attitude adjustment:

• **Be Well-Rested and Exercise Regularly.** Studies show that usually within five minutes after even moderate exercise, you'll get the benefit of an enhanced mood. Studies have also proven that even partial sleep deprivation has a significant negative effect on mood. If you feel better, you are better.

• **Play Uplifting or Energizing Music Before Your Calls or Meetings.** Whatever fires you up: rock or rap, country, gospel, it don't make no nevermind. My personal favorite: "It's a Long Way to the Top" by AC/DC. In *The Office*, nerdy salesman and Assistant to the Regional Manager Dwight Schrute blasts Mötley Crüe's "Kickstart My Heart" at full volume in his car to prepare for a sales meeting. This may or may not work for you.

• **Put a Smile on Your Face.** Studies show the power and impact of smiling. When you smile you convey happiness, confidence, and positivity. Smiling invites a connection with others, and it's contagious. Science to the rescue: it may sound ridiculous, but research shows that even forcing a smile onto your face for ten seconds can trick your brain into believing you're happy, resulting in actual feelings of happiness. This can boost your mood and immune system, lower stress, and possibly even make you live longer. (Not that I'm recommending Botox, but researchers also discovered that people unable to frown due to Botox injections were happier than those who could frown.)

Please take note: none of this is a myth or hyperbole. A positive attitude—by remembering the A in F.A.C.E. the Day—can help you *Carpe Diem, Carpe Noctem, Carpe Plurimum*: Seize the Day, Seize the Night, Seize the Deal!

(These tactics are also useful for bolstering your sales performance, so we'll be returning to them in future chapters.)

CHAPTER 4

F.A.C.E. THE DAY: CONTROL

EDibles: Control Variables to Reach Your Goals

"If you lose self-control, everything will fall."
—JOHN WOODEN

In full disclosure, in my own life I generally took my health for granted.

As a younger man, I was blessed or cursed with a tough constitution. For many years, booze, lack of sleep, and constant travel bounced right off me like a tennis ball. But that changed once I hit my early thirties. It felt as if I'd hit a wall.

Suddenly I was thirty pounds overweight, and hangovers became a real factor for the first time in my life. Taking control of my health was a big change and a big shift for me. When I started taking better care of myself, the results were immediate. I increased both my clarity and my energy. Both of those became big tools for improving my business success.

A major factor in gaining control over my health was a commitment to return to the gym. I recognize that the gym is not for everybody, but doing some form of exercise is crucial to feeling well and performing at your highest level. In my forties, I trained to become a Certified Personal Trainer (CPT) with the American College of Sports Medicine. I was coaching high-school rowing at our local boathouse, and due to the popularity of our program and the number of kids involved, a CPT was needed. Also we were based in New England, where the weather forces teams to spend a large part of the season indoors.

Wearing my CPT hat (not my salesman suit), I can testify that, regardless of what activity you go for—walking, jogging, cycling, rowing, surfing, basketball, Pilates, yoga, stand-up paddle-boarding—making sure that some regular block of time is dedicated to your fitness is imperative to maintaining control over your well-being. You don't need to run marathons or enter Ironman competitions.

Depending on your age, you might be more or less willing to listen to all this and consider your health as a factor in your success and happiness. Everybody's journey is different. I don't want to judge or preach. All I'm suggesting is to be present and aware of what's happening with your body and your mind. If your body runs better, you feel better, you work better. You can be more productive.

That said, I've always been a proponent of "everything in moderation"—including moderation...

F.A.C.E. the Day: Control: Putting the Principle into Play

"Control your own destiny. Or somebody else will control it for you."
—JACK WELCH

Ole Jack Welch was onto something with this whole **C**ONTROL idea. Controlling your own destiny is much preferable to the alternative.

But can you control all aspects of your destiny? Well, you can certainly aspire to take charge of many areas of your life, such as asking for a raise or choosing to change jobs. What you can control in your personal life isn't within the purview of this book, but we will discuss what aspects of your sales situation, and sales destiny, can be controlled—or at least what aspects you should aspire to control.

Let's begin by reviewing six of the most important aspects you can CONTROL: **Environment, Organization, Health, Preparedness, Pipeline,** and **Language**.

Control Your Environment. By making a solid plan and finding a quiet place where you can work on focusing on your goals, you can control your work and business environment. This level of control will bring consistency, structure, and results to your sales process. Everybody's mind needs stability and control.

Control Your Organization. Being organized can range from jotting down a "to-do" list on paper to creating elaborate spreadsheets. The five or ten minutes it takes to plan your day and set your targets will help you stay focused on each item until it's done; then that item can be crossed off your list. There are many organizational tools and calendar apps to choose from. Commit to one that suits your personality and makes staying organized easy, or even fun and fulfilling. My preference is good old-fashioned paper. I enjoy and get satisfaction out of crossing things off my list as I go through my day.

Control Your Health. Once again, I'll mention physical well-being as a component to effective sales. As far as exercise goes, I suggest a minimum of 400 kcals per day of any sort of exercise or activity, but please consult with your physician and/or personal trainer before starting any exercise program. You'll be astonished at the results that consistently oxygenating your body will bring. Diet and alcohol also play a role here. Some naïve notions of success paint a seductive picture along the lines of *The Wolf of Wall Street* (you have to party every night to be a success!). Don't fall for that cliché.

Control Your Preparedness. In business dealings, another important factor of being in control is being prepared. Be ready for uncertainty and the likelihood of unforeseen complications. At a minimum, for sales, this means being an expert in your field, carrying out due diligence before meetings with your clients, preparing stellar materials, and giving great presentations (all of which we'll cover in full detail in **Chapter 7: Due Diligence** and **Chapter 10: Presentation Skills**).

Control Your Pipeline. "How can the salesperson control what the clients do?" you may be asking. That's why this aspect of control may sound less feasible. But many techniques are at your disposal, and many kinds of communication, both internal and external, can be used to maintain some control over a deal as it progresses.

You can use clearly defined stages in your customer relationship management (CRM) system to keep track of where your clients are in the sales cycle. Each stage typically corresponds to how close you are to closing a particular deal—what's known as the "Probability of Close" (POC). By tracking what needs to be done at each stage, you can gain some control over the process. Here's an example of a "pipeline tracker" I might use:

Stage 1 (0% POC): Prospect identified but not yet contacted.

Stage 2 (10% POC): Customer contacted, materials sent.

Stage 3 (20% POC): Initial meeting or demo scheduled. Client agrees to meet or have a formal call.

Stage 4 (30% POC): Meeting or demo held.

Stage 5 (50% POC): Confirmed interest from client. Verbal commitment.

Stage 6 (75% POC): Documentation sent to the client.

Stage 7 (90% POC): Documents executed and completed by client.

Stage 8 (100% POC): Client onboarded. Deal closed.

Creating clear stages and being brutally honest with yourself and your management about where you stand with your prospect will ultimately lead to greater productivity. And the process will also give you a greater sense of CONTROL over your sales processes and business volume.

Control Your Language. Your use of language throughout the sales process is a critical component of managing a deal. By using tie-downs—getting commitments and confirmations along the way—you can stay in control of the situation. Rather than settling for a "send and wait" or "send and hope" strategy, impose realistic, reasonable, and agreed-upon mileposts. Then use specific language when communicating with your clients to move them along the pipeline and increase your control of the entire sales process. Here are some examples of language to employ at key stages:

• **Moving from Stage 1 to Stage 2:** Rather than asking, "When should I try you again?" say, "I'd like to send you some information on our product and services. How about I call you back in two weeks to discuss?" Or: "When should I follow up? Does two weeks sound right?" This utilizes both the classic "assumptive close" technique and implies a call to action. Don't be afraid to suggest the next milepost or logical step in the process. Most clients will respect the straightforward and practical approach. If not, they will probably let you know.

• **Moving from Stage 3 to Stage 4:** Say, "Thank you very much for your time and the discussion today. As a next step, we'd like to set up a demo of the system for you and your team. Do you have any time next week or the following?" You might try to be even more direct: "Is next week or the following better for a demo?" This is using "alternative close" language, asking not "if" they want a demo but "when" they want the demo.

• **Moving from Stage 4 to 5, or Stage 5 to 6:** Rather than asking, "Should I send some documents now?"—an approach that's too vague and soft—use a firmer tie-down, such as "Now that you've seen the demo and confirmed that this product can improve your situation, who is the best person on your team to review the documents?" Again, this is using the "assumptive close"—you're now speaking past the deal. When you ask, "Who should I send the documents to for review?" you're being assumptive; it's also an open-ended question that requires a reply.

Other examples of sales language that keeps you in control:

• **The Assumptive Close:** "Where are you going to park this car when you drive it home?" "Who is going to be the primary user of the system going forward?"

• **The Alternative Close:** "Do you want the blue one or the red one?" (Not "Do you want one?")

• **Speaking Past the Deal:** "We always send our new clients breakfast on their first trade. Would you prefer a Monday or Friday morning? Which is better for your team?"

• **Calls to Action:** "We'd like to schedule a call to review the documents with your legal counsel. Does Friday work?"

• **Logical Mileposts:** "If we get the accounts open by Friday, should we schedule training for late next week?"

All of these examples keep you in control of the process. Control is your friend, and it can also make the decision-making process easier for the prospect.

CHAPTER 5

F.A.C.E. THE DAY: EMPATHY

EDibles: Empathy Equals Opportunity

"Could a greater miracle take place than for us to look through each other's eyes for an instant?"
—HENRY DAVID THOREAU

Sometimes the power of empathy has surprised me.

In 2004 I was invited to London to speak at the Institutional Money Market Funds Association (IMMFA), the largest trade association representing the European money-market funds industry. The topic of my speech was the emergence of the money-market fund portal, which was still in its infancy. Unbeknownst to me, this conference would end up changing my life and altering the strategy for ICD.

My lucky break came when I spoke right after Conor Maher. Conor was a senior treasury officer from Hewlett-Packard and handled all of their global cash out of Bracknell, England. He spoke about HP's strategy of using offshore money funds. At the time they were running around $17 billion overnight, with approximately 21 different funds in their lineup. Their model, which required tons of liquidity, was one of the largest cash pools in the world. If you've ever bought an HP ink cartridge, you understand just how much cash they generate globally.

At the end of Conor's speech, he expressed his frustration

with managing 21 different funds. He then showed a slide showing a computer screen and a question mark, with the word "portal" below it. I was next on the stage, unable to believe my good fortune. ICD had developed the exact solution to the question that his slide had posed.

After my session, I went over and introduced myself to Mr. Maher, and asked if he would be willing to talk. He was up for it, and that's how our relationship began. Once the conference concluded, our conversation shifted to a pub and led to a very useful discussion. In our rapid-fire session, I learned the following:

• HP was using 21 funds, requiring numerous clumsy trading protocols: phone, fax, email, and various websites—all with substandard service and little appreciation for their business.

• HP was receiving 21 different reports, on different days, in various formats. This required many hours of work by his team to compile and aggregate all that data.

• The US-dollar money market world revolved around New York City and operated on Eastern Standard Time (EST), and he traded in London on Greenwich Mean Time (GMT). Nothing began until late in his day, approximately 14:00 GMT or 9:00 a.m. EST.

• Conor also told me, "I don't want to have lunch or play golf with money-fund reps. Please make them go away."

In my meeting with Conor, he allowed me to empathize with his situation and propose a solution. This solution was only relevant because I had ascertained his pain points. After I explained our model to Mr. Maher, I told him that our firm would do whatever it took to service his account, including working in his time zone. That piqued his interest. "Come into our offices and show me what you've got," he said.

After leaving the pub, my next call was to my business partners, Tom and Jeff. "Guess what?" I said. "I'm moving to London." The rest, as they say, is history.

I was in the right place at the right time when I met this life-changing individual. But listening to him and empathizing with his pain points gave us the opportunity to do business with him. In other words, empathy equals opportunity.

F.A.C.E. the Day: Empathy:
Putting the Principle into Play

"Empathy is about finding echoes of another person in yourself."
—MOHSIN HAMID

The final component of F.A.C.E. the Day is critical, and it's one that clearly separates the contenders from the pretenders: EMPATHY. It's also a tool that will help you use manners and etiquette to boost your sales performance.

Empathy is defined as the ability to understand or share the feelings of another.

Research has shown, perhaps predictably, that empathy makes people better, more caring, and more involved as family-members and friends. But did you know that empathy also makes people better managers and workers? Not only that, but empathy can be learned. According to the *New York Times*, researchers have discovered that, "far from being an immutable trait, empathy can be developed." That's good news for all you salespeople.

So how does empathy apply to sales? Ask yourself why, in the first place, you're even standing in the conference room. Sales empathy begins with understanding what problem you're there to solve.

Here's a common pitfall. Sales representatives often get so excited about their own product's clear superiority—superior in their own minds, that is—that they forget to relate their product back to the clients' needs. Whether it's a new car or a wireless plan, there's a big difference between selling and presenting "your" system, platform, or product and asking questions, meeting your potential client's needs, and selling them "their" next system. Empathize with your client's needs, and in all likelihood you'll soon find yourself developing, designing, or consulting with them to build their next product, service, or system.

When you're a sales empath, you consider the client's perspective:

• **Pain Points.** What "pain points" do they have today with their existing product, service, or system?

• **Goals.** What are their goals for their company's future, and what is the ideal end state for their problem?

• **Needs vs. Wants.** What are your client's needs, as opposed to their wants? What functionality or features are required, not just preferred?

• **Impact.** How will the client's decision to buy your product, service, or system impact their career or position in the firm?

From the start, you must try to put yourself in your prospect's position. For some individuals, choosing a product or a service for their company can be a career-defining decision. They don't want to mess it up. In considering your product, they must weigh many different factors, such as:

• **Existing Relationships.** What is their relationship with the competing vendor? Is it their lead bank? Are they a big customer? Are they a big shareholder?

- **Impact of Making a Change.** What are the efficiencies or complications gained or lost by making a change?

- **Cost.** Are there any new costs in making the change? Hidden costs? Potential savings?

- **Time.** What is the time and scope of implementation of the change?

- **Risk.** What is the potential reputational risk of making the wrong decision?

There's an old saying from the copier world: "Nobody ever got fired for buying a Xerox." This simply means that people or employees can avoid putting their jobs at risk by maintaining the status quo and choosing a well-recognized vendor. Compare that with the potential risk of choosing an upstart or unknown, even if the latter's product clearly appears better.

This paradigm applies to many, if not most, sales dynamics. Later on, in my career with ICD, "Big Banks," such as the Bank of New York or Goldman Sachs, served as the "Xeroxes" in my competitive landscape. It was clearly easier and less risky for a treasurer to award business to a Big Bank, because treasurers (and most people) felt more comfortable doing business with a known entity. Although the decision was often lazy and flawed, the existing relationship with the Big Banks—the treasurers' comfort zone—outweighed best practices.

In professional sales, you run into these sorts of conflicts all the time: which is more important to a prospect, a better product or a bigger corporate relationship? This is an area where having empathy for your customer and understanding their decision-making process can save you time and energy, if not help you win the deal. By being empathetic, mindful, and respectful of their situation, you'll ask better questions and get better information. This information will then enable you to advocate for your prospect and hopefully provide the logical path to your product.

That said, by using your sales empathy, it's also possible to learn that your value proposition does not move the needle. You may discover that the decision-maker is not going to buy either a Minolta or a Xerox, no matter what you do. In that case, it's better to ascertain this fact early and move on. One of the most significant attributes of a truly empathetic and professional salesperson is the ability to recognize the end of the line. When you're thinking, "This guy wouldn't buy a sweater from me if he were freezing to death," it's time to move on.

EMPATHY is the final piece of the F.A.C.E. puzzle. In my experience, being empathetic with your customers is the only way to earn clients for life. Short cuts and quick-buck artists will usually be thinned out of the herd in the long run.

Now let's begin our journey, prepared to F.A.C.E. the Day.

2

PREPARATION

CHAPTER 6

GREETINGS

EDibles: Fixing the Disconnect

"Do you think I could buy back my introduction to you?"
—GROUCHO MARX

You can feel the disconnection out there, despite all our efforts to connect.

Email, Facebook, texts, Twitter—it sure seems as if we're connecting. Yet these digital platforms often leave recipients feeling cold. Maybe it's because digital media aren't personalized or unique. They're only pixels. There's nothing to hold onto, nothing to touch and feel.

An email, while seemingly personalized, can still feel awfully impersonal. And an email newsletter or a tweet sent out to the masses, often to audiences of hundreds or thousands at a time, is even less distinctive. Even the telephone, while close to making you feel that you're "there" with someone, sometimes doesn't bridge the gap between people.

Once upon a time, we had a different way of connecting with each other—with a tip of the hat, a "Good morning," a handshake, a "Hello, my name is..." People lived at a different tempo in the days before the internet. Perhaps it's also because they went outdoors more frequently and could therefore give someone a personal and proper greeting, rather than being shackled to their computers.

How can we fix this disconnect? With one easy step: mastering the art of greeting another person. Face that person directly, when you can, and resist the temptation to hide behind your screen. An in-person introduction or handshake is intimate and exclusive. Gestures like these or a well-crafted note in your own handwriting (which we'll discuss in **Chapter 17: Handwritten Notes)** can help repair the divide between us and others.

People often tell me, anecdotally, that when they meet a business contact and that person makes eye contact with them, expresses appreciation for making their acquaintance, and is well-dressed for the occasion, they end up feeling that the meeting was significant and meaningful.

Can a hearty handshake, "It's a pleasure to meet you," and a gracious manner really serve as game-changers in a client's decision to do business with you? Probably not. But these little expressions of good manners never hurt. It's clearly better to be remembered for your courtesy than as "that dude from SunGard who puked after doing the ice luge in Denver."

Greetings: The Core Principle

"You can't shake hands with a closed fist."
—MAHATMA GANDHI

Some historians argue that the handshake started in medieval Europe, when knights would literally "shake" a stranger's hand as a way to shake loose any weapons hidden up their sleeve. In America, legend has it that the handshake was popularized by 18th-century Quakers, who wanted to democratize social interaction and cut through class and status by eschewing antiquated and submissive gestures like bows and curtsies.

Still, shaking hands, smiling, nodding, and introducing yourself remain deferential acts. You're not exactly bowing, but a solid greeting gives you the opportunity to pause and thank the other person for the honor of making their acquaintance. The ritual of a polite greeting is another kind of one-to-one communication, more personal and reflective of you—infused with your tone of voice, facial expression, smile, and touch—than an email or a voicemail can ever be.

The techniques in this chapter, as well as in **Chapter 17: Handwritten Notes,** "bookend" this book. Greetings form the beginning of any sales relationship, and a handwritten thank you note marks, not the end, but a transition to the later stages of the relationship. As this book's title suggests, there *is* no end to a successful business relationship. If you've followed my advice, the door with that client should always remain open.

Proper greetings and introductions, as well as the art of handwritten notes, also relate to the other techniques in this book, in that they help in establishing rapport, maintaining relationships, listening actively, and transferring enthusiasm. They're tools that enable you to interact with and make an impression on your important business contacts in a polite and mindful way. Notes and greetings, in fact, can be seen as the epitome of professional business etiquette.

Greetings: Putting the Principle into Play

"You never get a second chance to make a first impression."
—WILL ROGERS

Most people remember meeting someone important for the first time—their future boss, spouse, colleague, or mother-in-law—especially when that first meeting is an epic fail. But no matter who you're meeting, you should always make sure to nail the first impression, because you never know how it will impact your life in the future. Remember that an initial "meeting" via a phone call or an email doesn't count. When you're meeting in person (or, for that matter, "meeting" over Zoom), the stakes are higher. Here's a run-down of best practices to insure that your first meeting goes off without a hitch.

Dress

"It is easy to decide on what is wrong to wear to a party,
such as deep-sea diving equipment or a pair of large pillows,
but deciding what is right is much trickier."
—LEMONY SNICKET

How you dress can have a big impact on how you're perceived. "Projecting success and confidence starts with your appearance," says Robert Speer, my friend and an extraordinary salesperson for Local Flow Logistics. "Spend the money on a fine watch, shoes, or empowering accessories. You will feel better walking into a room, and, whatever the situation, you will rarely be punished for being overdressed. Regardless of your product, consider the person on the other side of the table seeing you for the first time and asking, 'Is this someone I want to do business with?'"

• **Do** keep in mind the sales or business context. Make sure you wear the right outfit for the occasion. You can go casual when hosting or attending a backyard cook-out, but don't wear your tracksuit to a black-tie event.

• **Do** remember that good grooming habits, such as a shave, a haircut, an appropriate amount of makeup, and good overall hygiene, are important.

• **Don't** be too informal. Even though the trend is moving toward a more informal dress code in workplaces, not just on "casual Fridays," if I'm asking someone to invest $100 million with my company, I'm not going to show up for a sales presentation in my flip-flops, Hawaiian shirt, and jeans (although that would be my preference). You're rarely going to get thrown out of a deal for being too formal, but you might wipe out for appearing too informal.

• **Do** abide by regional cultural standards. In Asia, for example, appearance and protocol are more important than in Silicon Valley, where someone might quip, "Dude, if you wear a tie in my office again, I'll cut it off."

Shaking Hands

"A firm, hearty handshake gives a good first impression,
and you'll never be forgiven if you don't live up to it."
—**P. J. O'ROURKE**

A handshake is a key element in forming a good first impression. It can be hard to know exactly what to do and say, but my generic advice is this: Just be who you are and use the greeting that feels natural for you. (See "Pandemic Protocols" on pages 57-59 for more thoughts on the handshake in the age of Covid-19.)

• **Do** shake hands when greeting someone—male or female—whether you've met them before or not. If you're sitting, stand up to shake someone's hand, regardless of gender. Shake hands again when saying good-bye.

• **Do** aim for the palm of the hand, land your handshake, and confidently shake from the elbow a couple of times. Don't hang on forever; make it last for three or four seconds max.

- **Do** use your right hand, but be alert if someone extends their left hand instead of their right; their right hand may be injured (or holding something).

- **Do** use the occasion to say the party's name, e.g., "Fantastic to meet you, Nancy!" (This will also help you remember the person's name.)

- **Do** be aware of and adapt to cultural differences. In some countries, such as Russia, shaking hands in a doorway or threshold is seen as unlucky.

- **Don't** grab for the fingers or squeeze too hard. I've been guilty of both.

- **Don't** leave a hand extended to you hanging in midair. Immediately reciprocate.

- **Don't** get too huggy or kissy. Don't give a business associate a "bro hug" or plant an "air kiss" unless you know the person well and have established a relationship in which you've been given the "all clear" for that move. Look for social cues, and be respectful.

Eye Contact

"Eye contact beats any conversation."
—CHRISTINA STRIGAS

When greeting people and shaking hands, eye contact is a great way to make a personal connection. Studies show that eye contact can make your words more memorable and help people notice you and remember you better.

- **Do** maintain adequate and consistent (but not creepy) eye contact.

- **Do** be animated, nod approval, and smile.

• **Do** maintain a proper distance and continue to engage in appropriate eye contact until the conversation has ended.

• **Don't** stare, but also don't let your eyes wander around the room or across the person you're engaging. You don't want a business prospect to feel uncomfortable: "Uh, Bob? My eyes are up here."

Introductions

"Two of the greatest predictors of success are the ability to say hello and the ability to say good-bye."
—ROBERT J. BRAATHE

Whether you're meeting someone in an office, at a bar, or at a sales "road show," learning how to address a business contact properly is a crucial skill to master.

• **Do** use the person's last name (and sometimes their first name too) when introducing yourself, unless you were initially introduced by first name. "Nice to meet you, Rashida Hamilton. My name is Harvey Manfrenjensenden." Or "Ms. Keita, I'd like to introduce to you Mr. Jones from our accounting department." Err on the side of formality and politeness before you slide into a more casual mode. Rarely can you be too polite. With a woman, to avoid having to choose among "Miss," "Mrs.," and "Ms.," use the person's first and last name, or default to using "Ms." (as I have been instructed to do by many female counterparts).

• **Do** continue to use the form of the name that was used when you were first introduced, until invited to do otherwise. I'll say "Peter Townsend" or "Mr. Townsend" until I hear cues or am told, "Please call me 'Pete' or 'Peter.'" Personally, I consider it inappropriate for a business associate to refer to me by my first name without my permission.

• **Do** say, "I'm sorry, I'm not sure how to pronounce your name properly," if you've forgotten how to pronounce it or have forgotten a person's name entirely.

• **Do** repeat the person's name in conversation to retain it in your memory. Try discreet remembering techniques, like saying the name to yourself three times, jotting it down, or (at an event or meeting) drawing a quick table diagram and writing the attendees' names alongside their seat locations. You can also use a mnemonic device like "Miller is my mother's maiden name" or "Müller = mull; this guy is quiet and thinks a lot." (As for "Manfrenjensenden," good luck.)

• **Do** provide anecdotes to help others remember names and jump-start the conversation. "Ms. Keita is our new Head of Sales. She just arrived in Boston from Reno." This provides an opening for someone to say, "Great, when did you start?" or "Oh, my uncle lives in Reno."

• **Do** use name tags, especially at larger events where you might have a dozen or more people in attendance. Consider adding "place of work" and "job title" to the tags, which can lead to conversation. Name tags ease stress in a room and give people an out when they forget a name. Your tag should be worn above the pocket on the right side of your shirt, blouse, or jacket. You want the person you're meeting to be able to make direct eye contact with you and see your name as you shake hands.

• **Do** exchange business cards. This gesture—exchanging cards—may be a dying art, but I'm a big fan of it as a way to help folks remember who I am. Personally I like the Asian style of the "two-handed hand-over," with the card facing the recipient. I feel like the message this sends is "My card is important to me, and I'm honored to hand it to you." This gesture also shows that you've done business outside the States.

• How you present your business card really does make a difference. My former Spanish teacher, Thomas Donato, from the Jesuit High School in Sacramento, always said he could predict the grade he'd give a paper by the body language of the student as they turned it in to him—whether they did so proudly, lackadaisically, sneakily, or—in my case one time—sheepishly (because I'd clearly cheated). The same goes for your business card. Present it to your client with pride and confidence.

• **Don't** say, "Hey, you" or "What's that name again?" if you forget how to address someone. Say, "I'm so sorry. I know we had the privilege of meeting before, but I've forgotten your name. My apologies. Can you please refresh my memory?"

Pandemic Protocols:
Greetings in the Age of the Coronavirus

"It's amazing how email has changed our lives. You ever get a handwritten letter in the mail today? 'What the—? Has someone been kidnapped?'" **—Jim Gaffigan**

We are creatures of habit. The time-honored handshake at the end of a meeting has always served as a symbolic closure, signaling, "Thank you, it was a pleasure, we are done, time to walk away."

Also, traditionally, in business interactions, non-sexual and friendly forms of physical contact—a handshake, a fist bump, a high five, a back pat, a shoulder squeeze, a touch on the shoulder, arm, or hand, an air kiss, a hug—have been ways to establish rapport, show your bond, demonstrate that you agree and are pay-ing attention, or express empathy.

Now, however, in the age of the pandemic, shaking hands is out and wearing a mask is in, which means that establishing a meaning-ful business relationship presents challenges. We're also becoming more accustomed to less business travel and fewer in-person meet-ings, and more business transactions happening via video confer-ences. These transitions can make us feel weird. Recently, when I've met with clients face-to-face, I've encountered an uncomfortable moment reminiscent of going on a first date. Do we shake hands or what? When a presentation or lunch is over, how can we end it formally? The awkwardness is worthy of a *Seinfeld* episode.

On top of that, since the #MeToo movement's important awareness-raising shift concerning workplace sexual harassment, any physical contact runs the risk of being misinterpreted. And one must be sensitive to non-Western cultures in which hand-shaking, eye contact, and introductions may be traditionally more formal or else frowned upon entirely.

Overall, I suggest being prudent. Be respectful of the culture and of the times, and err on the side of caution. Here are some ideas to navigate this new terrain:

• **Ask first.** Inquire of your prospect or client if they or their com-pany have a policy around handshakes and masks.

• **Be clean.** If you do shake hands, always bring hand sanitizer to your meeting, clean up right after your greetings, and again at the end of the meeting. You might consider who is in your team or office "bubble"—your closest associates—and reserve handshakes and skipping masks for interactions with them.

• **Mask up.** Always have a mask for yourself and a sealed, unused one for each guest, just in case.

• **Remember the eyes.** When wearing a mask, eye contact is more important than ever.

• **Verbalize more.** You may have to make up for the lack of a handshake by expressing aloud what you'd normally convey non-verbally, via physical contact.

In terms of replacing the handshake, office and professional culture already seems to be evolving. Here are some options for both greetings and departures:

• The elbow bump

• The bow, brief nod, or head tilt

• The Hindu "namaste" gesture: place your palms together, fingers up, and make a shallow bow with your head.

• The standard hand-wave

• Placing your right hand over your heart while making eye contact with the other person, as is often done in the Middle East

• The American Sign Language "thank you" gesture. With your dominant hand, raise your palm to your face, keeping it flat, with the fingers together. Starting with your fingers near your lips, move your hand out and downward in the direction of the other person.

Navigating all of these concerns is difficult, and the future of in-person connection and bodily contact—hugs, air kisses, handshakes, elbow bumps, etc.—remains uncertain. Customs will surely evolve, so stay tuned. Personally, I hope the awkward elbow bump does not last forever. You never know—we may be doing the funky-chicken dance soon.

CHAPTER 7

DUE DILIGENCE

EDibles: A Sales Navigator Gets Lost

> "I believe luck is preparation meeting opportunity.
> If you hadn't been prepared when the opportunity
> came along, you wouldn't have been lucky."
> —OPRAH WINFREY

Here's the scene. I'm in my office when I receive a cold email from an enterprise software sales rep at LinkedIn. Let's call him Bob the Vendor. Bob is pitching a product called Sales Navigator. LinkedIn, as you know, is the world's leading online social network for job-seekers and hiring managers, with over 600 million participants. Bob asks me, "Would you like to learn about the benefits of LinkedIn Sales Navigator?"

Before I tell you what happens next, have you ever heard of Sales Navigator? Some of you may know that it's a very slick sales management tool that helps sales reps tap into LinkedIn's massive network. Sales Navigator is also a coordinated look-through tool that allows teams to link all of their connections together. I can see my team's connections, they can see mine, and we can rank and position people within our LinkedIn network. It's a powerful instrument for any sales organization. With one click, I can see if somebody from LinkedIn has any connection to ICD. With two clicks, I can see who those connections are.

Back to ballsy Bob, who emailed me directly. At the time, I was not only the Co-Founder and CEO of ICD but also its Global Head of Sales. Have you ever made a cold call? If you have, you can appreciate the pain and anxiety it often causes for the salesperson. You can also appreciate the jubilation that person will feel if the cold call results in an actual lead or other successful outcome. At the time I figured that this email from Bob the Vendor was a blast email, and that he must have a terrible hit rate. Besides, his sales pitch wasn't very good. But I replied anyway: "Sure, I'd love to hear about Sales Navigator." We set up a conference call. (I was imagining Bob picking himself up off the floor, having fallen from pure shock after getting a response to his uninspired email.) After the call, we set up an in-person meeting in New York.

LinkedIn's offices are in the Empire State Building. I went to the meeting, and Bob seemed prepared. He'd clearly researched my profile and learned a few things about myself and my business dealings. He made polite chitchat with me: "I see you lived in London. I see you played rugby. I see you're into personal training." He got good marks on all of these points.

Then, when I asked him if he'd ever heard of our company, ICD, he said he had looked at our website and understood what we did: short-term liquidity investments for corporations. But he hadn't dug deep enough to find out who our clients were and what our relationships with them were like. If he had, he would have discovered that his own company, LinkedIn, was one of ICD's biggest clients at that time. Hence the reply from a CEO. Because when a big-ass customer calls me up to ask if I'm interested in their product, you know what my answer is? "Yes. I will definitely consider your product. You have considered mine."

The biggest irony of all? With two clicks, using his own product, Sales Navigator, Bob the Vendor could have seen our firm's senior vice president's connection to his treasurer and CFO. Using his own tool, or even just some clever legwork through other means, he could have understood the relationship of my firm to his and why I returned his email so readily.

I was being polite. Bob the Vendor, not so much. In the end, his sales pitch wasn't a total wipeout. He got the deal, and Sales Navigator proved to be a very effective product. But poor Bob had not done his due diligence before sending his first email, or even before setting up our meeting. He got an "A" on finding out my personal information but an "F" on researching my company's information.

This was an eye-opening experience for me. I use this story with my own sales reps when I talk about the importance of due diligence. I tell them that, first, you should know what a prospect's company does. Second, you should explore any mutual connections. Third, you should figure out if you're currently doing business, or if there's an opportunity for potential business that you can do together by leveraging these connections. Everybody likes to do business with people who do business with them. And who knows—if it's your client, maybe the CEO, treasurer, or purchasing agent will take your cold call.

Don't miss out. Be prepared. Don't make a dumb-ass mistake. It's like walking into the lobby of Coca-Cola in Atlanta, hoping to make a sale, while drinking a Pepsi. Do your homework.

Due Diligence: The Core Principle

"I will prepare, and someday my chance will come."
—ABRAHAM LINCOLN

According to the dictionary, "due diligence" in a business sense means "the research and analysis of a company or organization done in preparation for a business transaction." Yes, you need to do that: scope out a client or prospect before your first interaction, in order to be a better-informed salesperson and ensure that you can solve the client's problems.

But I also view due diligence in a more unexpected way. To me, due diligence is a way of showing manners and respect. It's the first step to polite and professional sales, and the first component of every salesperson's skills. By this I mean that performing due diligence must happen before you do anything else. In essence, polite and professional conversation—and professional sales—boils down to these points:

• Understanding your audience

• Understanding the company you're calling

• Understanding the person you're calling, their position or job, and their needs

Carrying out due diligence properly is a kind of art. You want to be prepared but not over-prepared. You want information about your client but not so much that you seem creepy or stalker-ish. To be sure, how you perform research and analysis has changed a lot because of the internet. In the past, you couldn't google someone's name and see everything that's happened to them since they were twelve. Gathering advance information was still done before the internet— you could look up a company and find its financials—but the data wasn't instantaneous, and it came from other resources: newspapers, trade journals, magazines, networking. Now you type in a company's or person's name, and everything appears on Yahoo Finance; you get their entire employment history in a blink of an eye.

The Three Purposes of Due Diligence

"Opportunity does not waste time with those who are unprepared."
—IDOWU KOYENIKAN

However you perform the necessary research to become prepared, good due diligence has three distinct purposes:

1. Showing Respect. Due diligence shows respect to your prospects. You've put in work that shows you appreciate their valuable time. You understand who they are, what they do, what their position, role, and responsibilities are, and what their organization or company does. You can demonstrate that you've connected with the right person, and that (hopefully) you can speak their vernacular.

2. Creating Empathy. Due diligence also shows that you've tried to identify their problem. Knowing the problem in advance will help you understand, once you're on the phone or in the room with them, (1) What issue or problem you are there to fix or solve, and (2) How can you help them do their job more efficiently and effectively. These aims are also expressions of empathy: "I'm here to listen and help."

3. Finding a Connection. Due diligence can help you find a connection with this person. Through such channels as LinkedIn, Google, Facebook, Instagram, and Twitter, you might find out that you've got something in common with the person—a mutual friend or acquaintance, a past place of employment, a hometown, an alma mater, an organization, a church, a personal interest or hobby, you name it. Do your homework and jot down what you find. Connections, even those that emerge from remote places, can help facilitate dialogue and enhance rapport. When you're finally talking in person, find ways to weave in those details and watch how they brighten the room and break the ice.

Without respect, empathy, and prior knowledge, there's much less likelihood of forming a genuine business engagement. It may happen anyway, but the likelihood for successfully connecting becomes haphazard or random. Due diligence increases the chances that you'll find a connection, and therefore increases your chances of forging a useful business relationship. Without preparation and due diligence, you haven't earned the necessary respect to go further.

Due Diligence: Putting the Principle into Play

> "Research is the highest form of adoration."
> —**PIERRE TEILHARD DE CHARDIN**

In my experience, due diligence pays off. It paves the way for polite and professional communication, which in turn helps you earn the right to take the next step with the prospect and gain their business. That first step toward polite and professional communication should begin well before you pick up the phone or craft an introductory email.

Here are four ways to perform good due diligence on a client or a prospect:

1. Go Beyond Top-Level Information. So you've ascertained that Ms. Khan is VP of Sales and Commercial Operations for a company, and that she likes classical guitar and beekeeping. Now that you've got her permission to make a sales pitch or take a meeting, add a second level of research to make this client feel that you understand her problems and what she needs. Discover the kinds of products and solutions that might interest her.

The key is using open-ended questions that will get a person talking:

- What is an example of an excellent vendor relationship?
- What does "great customer service" mean to you?
- What is the best product you ever bought, and why is it the best?

The answers to questions like these will tell you volumes about the person you are dealing with and how your sales relationship can best serve them.

2. Research Comps. It's a very common practice, when you walk into a client meeting, to talk about the product or service you're currently providing to a similar company, even a competitor of theirs. For example, if you have a meeting with Dell Computers, you might say, "You know, we deal with several large tech companies, and we're very familiar with the space." In a meeting with Honeywell, you might say, "Your situation isn't dissimilar to one I dealt with at Tyco. Would it be helpful if we solved the problem for you the way we solved it for them?" Like people, companies emulate those in similar positions, and they value their connections to industry colleagues. Understanding comparable organizations, or "comps," is an important facet of performing due diligence.

3. Find Community References. Atlanta, where both Delta Airlines and Home Depot are headquartered, provides a great example of what I mean by "community references." When I travel there to talk to Delta, I keep in mind that one of the reasons I'm meeting with them in the first place is that Home Depot is also one of my clients. Delta wants to know how the biggest company in town, the one with the brightest, shiniest, strongest treasury organization, is operating. "What the heck is Home Depot doing?" they may ask. "Tell me about Home Depot's best practices."

I might say, "I'm happy to explain their criteria and decision-making process. In fact, if you'd like to speak to some of our local clients, I'd be happy to set that up. Would you be interested in talking to Coca-Cola, Home Depot, or Southern Company?" Researching community references and a company's community standing so that you can use that information in a sales pitch or meeting is another important facet of due diligence. When your clients are selling for you, it's the best of all worlds.

(An important reminder: be sure to have the permission of your other clients before you use them as references.)

4. Use Flattery and Information As a Foot in the Door. You're going to attract more flies with sugar than with salt. And if you're being courted, it's good to know that the person who wants to do business with you has done their homework and has flattering things to say about your career and accomplishments. After performing due diligence to investigate a prospect, praise their work or position in the company, or name-drop the network of their peer organizations or colleagues.

You might say, "Here in your community, we do business with Coca-Cola, Home Depot, and UPS. Are you familiar with any of those guys? Do you happen to know any of their treasury professionals? Matt from Home Depot? Melissa from Coca-Cola? Maria from UPS? Of course you do. You're a true player in this community."

Here's another example. One of my reps pays attention to the financials, stocks, and press releases from any company that he's pitching and uses that information as his foot in the door. When he sees the stock go up on a company like Cigna or Aon, he'll reach out and say, "Hey, I see your stock was up five bucks. I just wanted to call and congratulate you on a great quarter. I'd love to talk to you about what you guys are doing with your cash, and help you maximize your returns there." He uses his smarts and carries out savvy due diligence to show that he's following the company and is up to date on its latest news. That's another form of flattery, and it shows good business manners.

Due Diligence: Don't Try This

"Learning is not attained by chance, it must be sought for with ardor and diligence."

—ABIGAIL ADAMS

Due diligence is about doing your homework. Sometimes that homework can serve as your foot in the door, and the layers of due diligence can evolve as you progress through the deal. But can too much research be overkill? Can it feel a little stalker-ish? Yes. So here are some parameters to keep in mind:

1. Avoid Getting Too Personal Too Fast. Some people don't want to discuss their personal lives in any way, shape, or form. Respect this. (Please see the "Fire your loins" story in **Chapter 10: Presentation Skills.**)

2. Maintain a Personal/Business Social Media Firewall. Resist checking out the personal social media profiles (on Facebook, Instagram, etc.) of your prospects. Keep your research above board (on LinkedIn or Google, for example) and on a professional level. Avoid personal details like "I saw your vacation to Cabo on Facebook" until you've developed a relationship.

3. Steer Clear of Conversation Killers. Maintain no-fly zones for topics of conversation that involve politics and religion. Unless you're selling to a church or politician, of course...

4. Don't Be Dishonest. It sounds obvious, I know, but don't make up false connections. Don't say, "Hey, I see we both went to Harvard!" or "I'm a big fan of Coca-Cola. In fact, I've been a shareholder since Warren Buffett told me about it in 1987." (Unless these statements are true.) If you and your potential client both went to Harvard, then you've genuinely got some common ground. If the company you're pitching is one you're genuinely fond of and you're a shareholder, great. As I've said, people like to do business with people who do business with them. But don't misrepresent yourself; it could come back to haunt you.

5. Beware of Paralysis by Analysis. Sometimes people fool themselves into believing they're working hard on due diligence when in fact they're overthinking every move. It's not important to know why the phone works before you dial it. Set a time-frame for due diligence, work through it, and then stop and begin talking to the clients and prospects. With the right questions, you'll learn much more from them in the flesh than you ever could online.

CHAPTER 8

ESTABLISHING RAPPORT

The "Fabulous Five" Versus "Ten Things That Require Zero Talent"

"You can make more friends in two months by becoming interested in other people than you can in two years by trying to get other people interested in you."
—DALE CARNEGIE

We all know, or can at least recognize, people who operate with great social ease. They're smooth, charismatic, comfortable—and other people like to be around them. To these interesting, engaging, "life of the party" types, we often attribute a group of characteristics. The most typical of these we'll call the "Fabulous Five" traits:

1. Being good-looking

2. Being gregarious and charming

3. Being funny and approachable

4. Being an expert in their field

5. Being confident

While these are all admirable traits, they're not necessarily required to establish rapport and build relationships. Besides, most of us are not blessed with all of these "Fabulous Five" traits. Some of us, if we're lucky, can muster a couple of them, in spurts, given a particular situation. The rest of us are most likely zero or one for five, on a good day.

Fortunately, there's still hope for folks like us. I've discovered a different set of fundamentals that can help us establish rapport. And, thankfully, these can be learned and earned by anyone.

Before we get to that, let me tell you about the power of having no talent. Yes, you heard me right. One of my favorite internet sensations was an article called "10 Things That Require Zero Talent," which made the rounds some years ago. Though many have taken credit for writing it, its author is unknown. One rumor claims that it was penned by a high-school football coach on a whiteboard in a locker room. All I know is that I've walked into people's offices and seen this list up on their wall:

10 Things That Require Zero Talent

1. Being on time
2. Work ethic
3. Effort
4. Body language
5. Energy
6. Attitude
7. Passion
8. Being coachable
9. Doing extra
10. Being prepared

My point in comparing the "Fabulous Five" traits to the "10 Things That Require Zero Talent" is this: if you're not blessed with more than one or two of the "Fabulous Five"—which, to be honest, is a ridiculous list of rare and mostly innate attributes—don't sweat it. We can't all be George Clooneys or Tony Robbinses or Beyoncés.

But this other set of ten fundamental skills you *can* learn and earn, and they will also help you connect with others, as long as you put in some attention and hard work and are open to doing things differently. These skills can set you apart and prepare you for success. We can learn to be on time, or improve our body language, or do a better job being prepared, or even have a better attitude. Even if some of these skills come naturally to us, we still need to be aware of them, so that we can call upon them at will and understand how to use them in the right situations.

The same goes for establishing rapport. Like many of the techniques and tactics in this book, building rapport is a skill that can be learned. Let's get to it.

EDibles: Tom, JJ, and Ed: A Tale of Three Partners

> "There are friends, there is family, and then
> there are friends that become family."
> **—ANONYMOUS**

I've been fortunate enough over the course of my career to work with and learn from many outstanding individuals who are mentioned in this book. In particular, I had the great fortune to start a business with two individuals who both had the "Fabulous Five" attributes and allowed me to "draft" off their skills—like drafting in car-racing, when the lead car displaces the air behind it and actually pulls a second car in its wake.

By far the best two "rapport and relationship" salespeople I've ever met are my former partners from ICD, Tom Newton and Jeff "JJ" Jellison. The three of us, personality and style-wise, complement each other nicely. Tom and JJ are like brothers to me. Brothers may fight sometimes, but they always end up around the fireplace at Christmas. (That's another story.) In some ways, though, as guys and salesmen, we couldn't be any more distinct.

JJ is a "them, those, aw shucks" kind of guy. He operates with a warmth, humility, and affable humor that make it impossible not to love him. He's like a cross between a golden retriever and Samuel Clemens: lovable and loyal, with a simple wisdom and life outlook. He's also a Derek Jeter type: handsome, a remarkable athlete, a scholarship baseball player, and seemingly able to play anything well: rugby, volleyball, ping pong. JJ competes in everything he does like an absolute monster.

Tom is more raw and charismatic, but he's not afraid to break people in half (in a good way). He operates with an intoxicating mix of charm and confidence. I'd call him a perfect hybrid of Robert Redford, Jack Nicklaus, and Santa Claus—an outstanding actor, participant, and director who showers people with gifts and praise and feels jolly about it. I've watched him do it hundreds of times. His manner is not trite or phony, it's genuine. Plus, Tom is a remarkable golfer.

As for myself, I'd say I'm the comedic relief of the team. And I have a few other redeeming qualities that I'll try to reveal over the course of the book.

I'll tell you, it's been something to watch and learn from Tom and JJ. I've borrowed more techniques from those two guys than from all of my other business colleagues combined. Many of the techniques shown in this chapter I owe to them.

Establishing Rapport: The Core Principle

"Rapport is the ability to enter someone else's world, to make him feel that you understand him, that you have a strong common bond."
—TONY ROBBINS

What is the goal of establishing rapport and maintaining a business relationship? In other words, what are you trying to achieve? Is it about getting clients to trust you? Is it about getting them to like you? It's certainly about building trust and building a relationship, instead of letting your relationship remain merely at the vendor/ consumer level.

Here's a big reason why you want to create good rapport. Nobody likes to be sold something. Nobody likes to raise their hand and say, "Wow, I was really *sold* on that." People much prefer to *buy* things.

If your product is markedly inferior to your competitor's product, then it may not matter how hard you work to ingratiate yourself to your client. But if the products are all pretty close, within several degrees of price or efficacy—and in my experience, usually only a few degrees separate any two high-quality products—then personal preference plays a large part. That's when establishing rapport to create a strong relationship will play a big role.

A business relationship can exist at three different levels:

• **Level 1: Purely professional.** This type of relationship exists at the level of "good morning, good afternoon." Your relationship never leaves the office or the phone.

• **Level 2: More personal.** At this stage, you can take the relationship to a slightly more intimate level. You'll meet in person, spend some time together, get to know each other personally.

- **Level 3: Friendship.** At this stage, you'll dine together, wine together, and engage in entertainment, like taking the client to a sporting event, the theater, a charity event, and so forth. If you do something social with them—it may not even be business-related—then you've begun to stray toward pure friendship. This is the Holy Grail, the ultimate stage of relationship to aspire to, in which you'll gain a friend as well as a client.

Over the years, I've managed a lot of young salespeople. What I tell them is that you have to maintain a long-term perspective. You have to assume that your prospect, client, or customer is potentially going to be dealing with you, and you with them, for weeks, months, years, or even the rest of your professional career. I teach them that a business relationship is more than transactional. You don't deal with a client once. You're hoping to deal with them forever. Instead of "BFF"—"best friends forever"—I like to talk about "BCF"—"best clients forever."

Establishing rapport is beneficial for both the salesperson and the client. It allows the salesperson to understand the client's situation: their true concerns, their needs, and what problems the salesperson can solve for them. And rapport benefits the client because they will gain not only the product but also, possibly, a friend or valuable business relationship.

As a salesperson, you need to get inside a customer's head to understand why they're talking to you in the first place. If you can turn your dealings with that client into a relationship, or even a friendship, then you can understand them far better. In this chapter, we're going to talk about how to use some fundamental tools of manners and etiquette to do just that.

Establishing Rapport: Putting the Principle into Play

"The stronger the relationships, the stronger the business,
the higher the satisfaction levels in all involved."
—**CONNIE LINHART, RETIRED, FORMER CFO, LORILLARD**

As I said above, establishing a friendly, trustworthy rapport with your prospect or potential client provides them with an opportunity to *choose* your product, not be sold on it. But in order to do that, you need to earn the right to ask for their business. Here are some specific steps and techniques that harness the power of manners and etiquette to establish rapport.

Your first step is to engage your prospect or potential client in a dialogue—ideally in person or on the phone—that's inviting and opens the possibility to form a connection. But what do I really mean by "inviting"? Let's break that down and explore some examples of how to use polite, professional dialogue to invite the building of rapport.

1. Empower Your Client: Let Them Drive the Bus. An empowering dialogue assigns power to the person you're speaking with. In conversations, you confer authority by assigning the other person credit or accolades, or by giving them control. You don't want to compliment them on their appearance (that's a no-no). But with a few choice phrases, you can let them know that they're an important and knowledgeable person, that you respect their position, and that you're respectful of their time and expertise. That's the concept of empowerment: let them know that they're in control. They're driving the bus, and you're the humble passenger.

For example: "You know, Mary Ann, I understand the position you're in. I respect your job and the importance of it, and I want to be very respectful of your time. I also understand that you must speak to a lot of salespeople and hear a lot of offers providing different solutions. So I'm going to be mindful of that and try hard not to waste your limited time."

When you use this technique to assign the other person power, they will immediately feel that they're being treated with respect in the conversation. They will gain the sense that they're in control. And once they feel that they're in the driver's seat, you'll have better access to information that will help you improve their situation.

As we discussed, nobody wants to be sold anything. But everybody is willing to buy something if they feel empowered. Assign your client the power, and pay respect to their portion of the conversation.

2. Show Preparedness and Inquisitiveness: More Listening Than Talking. This means, first and foremost, being well-versed in your subject, your product, and your client or prospect's needs.

It also means being able to engage in polite and friendly, honest, non-threatening dialogue, which will allow you to qualify the customer to buy your product. If you're getting honest, unfettered access to their world, then true persuasion can take place. But if the person's guard is up—if they feel defensive or suspicious of you and your motives—then they're not going to tell you much. They're just going to try to get you to leave them alone.

You can also build rapport by being respectful and exceedingly courteous. Have you heard the old expression "Everything you say before 'but' doesn't matter"? For example, "Ed, you're a tall and handsome, good-looking guy, *but* you've got terrible breath." Being exceedingly courteous and showing curiosity are much better tactics than rushing to speak and perhaps being accidentally insulting by adding a regrettable *but*. "Mr. Jones, I recognize you've got five minutes and you're a really important guy, *but...*" Instead of taking that route, be inquisitive and listen. Remember, you're there to solve a problem or improve a situation for somebody.

You might say, "So let me understand your current situation," or "Tell me about the system you're using right now." Using an example from my own career, I might say, "Mr. Jones, how do you buy your money funds now?" In reply, Mr. Jones might say, "Well, we pick up the phone," or "We randomly search multiple websites," or "We use a broker."

This dialogue does two things: It helps to establish rapport with the client or prospect, and it helps me understand the situation more fully. The information I gain from this dialogue helps me filter my message and determine where I'll go next—the logical path that leads to my product.

3. Look for Cues: Another Form of Listening. This technique comes into play when you're meeting somebody in person. What does it mean when you're talking to someone and they're smiling or joking, or when you see them in a welcoming posture, leaning back in their chair, arms open, their hands turned upward? How does that differ from someone who is reserved, arms crossed, sitting ramrod straight in their chair, a frown on their face?

Look at the way your client or prospect is sitting at the table. Are they leaning forward with both hands on the table? Are they leaning back and peering through their glasses? If they offer positive cues—an open posture, laughter, leaning forward, and so forth—you can feel confident that they're welcoming your pitch, and you can be friendlier.

After receiving this all-clear signal, you might begin to have more fun with the contact. Go ahead, veer off the stiff path of the Fuller Brush Man routine. There's a time to be proper and polite, and there's also a time to be more informal, as long as you allow the client to open the door for that shift.

Mirroring your customer is an opportunity. Physically and emotionally, a salesperson wants to be part of the yin and yang, the give and take, the body language, the kinetics in the room. You're subtly trying to break down walls that, in many office environments, are reinforced with concrete and rebar. So look for those positive cues and respond accordingly—but keep it short and professional, and get it over with quickly so that they have a pleasant experience and you can move on to the next dance.

What do you do if the positive cues aren't there? Don't say, "Oh, is that your golden retriever in that picture on the wall?" Bad move. If the music isn't right, finish the song quickly and move on. I've gone into meetings and realized quickly that the potential client is distracted and grumpy—they've had a bad morning, they're thinking about their next meeting, they're pissed off at something, maybe at the whole world. In that case I'll say, "Well, listen, we'll keep this really brief. I've got this product, and I'd like to show it to you. What do you think would be a better time to do that?" Then get the hell out of there, so that they know you took their cues.

4. Ask for Advice and/or Recommendations on the Way Out.
Elaborating on the potential "bad vibes" scenario in the previous step, let's say it's clear that you're not connecting with your client, for whatever reason. As a last-ditch effort, you might ask them how to proceed: "Ms. Smith, I can see you've got a lot going on today, and I want to be respectful of your time. I'm going to keep this really quick so that you can get back to tackling your issues of the day. But if you were in my shoes, what would you suggest as the next step here? So I can remain respectful of you and your timeline."

This also circles back to empowerment. Asking advice is an

empowering move and confers respect. With most people, this gesture will bring down their defenses. In all likelihood, instead of being a grump, they'll say, "You know what? You're right. Call me back in a week, and I promise I'll have more time for you." Or "Call me back in a month, when I can give this my attention." Or even the dreaded "You know, this is something we're probably just not going to do right now." At least you have a clear answer.

With a simple and polite request for advice and recommendations, you'll be surprised by how quickly you can sometimes turn the tide. And if you've flown halfway across the country to meet with them, even better. Guilt works. That said, it's pretty rare to travel thousands of miles for nothing but a firm "No thanks." Most people will have the decency to put you out of your misery before you've gotten on an airplane.

5. Ask Open-Ended Questions That Will Get Them Talking. Once you've established that a person does have time for you and there's an opportunity for a second conversation, whether it's on the phone or in person, ask questions, not only to make nice but to keep gathering information about your contact.

In a perfect sales call, you'll ask ten questions and never say anything. If you ask well-phrased questions, you're leading prospects down the logical path to buying your product, which is your sales *raison d'*être.

Here are some examples of open-ended questions to get your prospects and clients talking:

• **"What are the biggest challenges you face?"** This question works for every human in every discussion, and there is no time when you can't ask it. (Another, less formal version might be "What's the biggest pain in your ass?")

• **"If you could design a perfect system in a perfect world, what would this system do for you?"** or **"Tell me, what's the least favorite functionality you have to deal with right now?"** These are other ways of opening a conversation about the challenges they face and the problems you can solve. Ideally, the thing you're proposing, your solution or product, is going to solve these problems. In a perfect world, you'll know that before you get in the room.

• **"So, Mr. Garcia, what sort of trading systems have you used? Tell me a little about the challenges you have with your system today."** Ask open-ended questions like these that relate to your product. The client will probably reply with useful information: "We don't like the reporting, it's not a very good website, the user interface isn't very good, we struggle with data flow because it's not integrated with my system." Open-ended questions will get them talking.

• **"Of all the vendors you deal with, who is your favorite and why? We want to be like them."** Once you know the answer to this question, ask, "Who are your least favorites and why? No names—just tell me why you don't like them."

• **"How long have you been at the company?"** This is an easy conversation-starter.

• **"Tell me a little about your career path"** or **"your time at this firm"** or **"where you went to school."** Prior to speaking with them, you can also look for commonalities, either from their company profile or by doing a Google search or LinkedIn search on their background. Then, in person, you can ask questions about those connections. (This technique is discussed in more depth in **Chapter 7: Due Diligence.**)

• **"Let me tell you about the time..."** For your half of the conversation, try this tactic: share a family story or a funny industry story that might brighten up the room, or offer a few personal facts about yourself. Plenty of small-talk topics are safe: pets, kids, sports, hobbies—anything that could trigger a connection.

6. Express Gratitude for the Opportunity. This one may be obvious, but a simple expression of gratitude goes a long way toward establishing rapport. And it can be that simple. Some key phrases you can use to express gratitude:

• **"Thank you for your time."**

• **"I know your time is limited and precious, and you're a busy person."** If this is said in a genuine way, people sense it, and the elaboration can be more effective than just saying thank you.

• You can even take it a step further: **"I genuinely appreciate your time and this opportunity. It means the world to us, and we won't let you down. I recognize that any system or product you choose is a career decision, so I'm not taking that lightly. Thank you for entering into this discussion. You know, we're 100-percent cognizant of your position and your responsibility."**

• Send thank you messages along the way, either an email or a handwritten note after each meeting. You can also connect on LinkedIn. (More details on these techniques are covered in **Chapter 6: Greetings; Chapter 13: Phone; Chapter 14: Email; Chapter 15: Social Media;** and **Chapter 17: Handwritten Notes.**)

Establishing Rapport: Don't Try This

"Take chances, make mistakes. That's how you grow."
—MARY TYLER MOORE

Here are a few *faux pas* and blunders to avoid as you establish rapport with a client. Some of these examples are mistakes I've already made, so you don't have to. (You're welcome.)

1. Foot-in-Mouth Disease. Some topics should be kept off-limits or held for later in the relationship. Be careful not to get too personal or chummy too fast, or you might risk a complete wipe-out.

2. Getting Ahead of Myself. Let's say you've just gotten out of a meeting that you think has gone well. You seem to have truly connected with the person, and they seem interested in your product. But you don't want to come on too strong. You want to establish rapport, not show too much enthusiasm and scare them away. Or for that matter, seem inappropriate.

The obvious (boneheaded) thing to do would be to send a billion texts or emails immediately, or invite them out for a celebratory drink that same day. A more realistic danger might be that you've received an early indication of interest and think things are going so well that you ought to send your paperwork the next day, without their permission. But this can backfire. You don't want to race ahead in the process without politely obtaining permission to take that next step.

3. Going Over or Around Their Head. You should never go over the head of a potential client and attempt to deal with their boss instead, or go around them to other people in their organization.

That's suicide. If you trample on your main recommender, you will definitely not get the deal. Most conscientious superiors would refer you back to the recommender, but by then you'll probably already be dead to them. That said, sometimes you'll deal with people who are recommenders but not decision-makers. In that case you've got to dance the dance, but recognize that sometimes you'll lose by not dancing with the decision-maker.

4. Being Disingenuous. Be natural, be respectful, and be yourself—just don't go overboard. You don't want to come off like Eddie Haskell on *Leave It to Beaver.* You may not be old enough to know that old TV show from the 1950s, but Eddie was one of those self-serving guys who everybody knew was just sucking up all the time. Even the parents knew. His technique was so blatantly obvious, you couldn't help but think, "Eww, don't get any of that on me." Remember, you can be friendly and chatty without being an ass-kisser.

3
PERFORMANCE

CHAPTER 9

MAINTAINING RELATIONSHIPS

EDibles: Aiming for the Ten-Year Deal

"Stay connected. Most people move through the stages
of their life shedding groups of friends as their geography,
circumstances, or workplaces change. Ed is a connector and
works hard to maintain his extensive network of friends,
friends of friends, clients, etc. Nothing bad is ever going to
come from knowing and liking a large group of people."
**—RUSS DRIVER, FORMER DIRECTOR
OF DEUTSCHE ASSET MANAGEMENT**

Some deals that I've spearheaded have taken ten years to pay off.

It's not that I would constantly call the clients and leave increasingly desperate voicemails for a decade. Even I'm not that persistent (or crazy). What I mean is this: I've watched and waited and worked patiently as a lucrative business relationship has evolved, developed, and matured over time. I've learned that it pays to be patient.

Remember those Friday nights spent standing uselessly at the back of the gymnasium at the high-school dance? You have to dance with a lot of partners. You have to endure rejection. Above all, you have to keep dancing, remembering that sometimes the last one dancing wins the game.

When you move this analogy from the realm of tragic teenage

romance to the world of business, the same principles apply. With some potential clients, you end up maintaining a long-term relationship with them as they move from one company to the next. This phenomenon is typical in many industries, especially in my prior business, the treasury space. You might begin dealing with an employee who's in purchasing at, for example, Apple. Two years later, that employee might transition from Apple to Google, then leave Google to land at Cisco. This kind of career movement provides opportunities for you to add new clients, because you already know this employee. I can think of multiple examples of folks I've done business with who, over the past twenty years, have worked at five different companies. This means that they've been clients of mine not once or twice but three to five times, because we've continued our relationship as business associates, and eventually as friends, throughout the evolution of their careers.

"Don't celebrate closing a sale; celebrate opening a relationship."
—PATRICIA FRIPP

You want to build a strong relationship not only in case a client goes to another company, but also in case they stay for years at the same one. In some large companies, people may stay put for their entire working lives. Others may transition frequently within an organization. It's an advantage to develop long-term relationships in all of these scenarios. Imagine you're a young restaurateur with big dreams of operating your own fancy bistro someday. First you need to scrub pots as the dishwasher; then you need to move onto the floor as a busser, then become a waiter. You'll do your time in the kitchen, as a sous chef and then a chef. Or you might become a sommelier or maître d'. Only then, with this breadth of experience under your belt, can you run the restaurant.

The same principle applies to the corporate world. If Margaret is working at ABC Company and eventually wants to become Head Honcho of Treasury, she's going to need to work in all ten areas of finance and treasury over the next twenty years to get there—first as a treasury analyst, then as a senior analyst, then as a director of treasury, and finally as a vice president & assistant treasurer. She might also work in sales, or operations, or marketing. And in each case, you can follow her career.

Furthermore, as you advance through your career, you're not likely to be in the same position forever yourself. As you move from one job to the next, you're going to meet dozens if not hundreds of potential business associates. And each time you move to a new company or climb up the corporate ladder, you can leverage those relationships all over again. But this can be done only by building long-term, lasting business relationships, or even friendships, over time. That's the key. As in a marriage or serious romantic relationship, in a business relationship you're in it for the long haul. Or, at least, you should be.

This is the focus of this chapter: how to maintain a relationship with a client you've worked hard to land, and with whom you've established a solid rapport. You're building the relationship with the person, not the company, because you know they may not be at the same company forever, and you might not be at your company forever. You want to keep upping your opportunities to sell them something, again and again and again.

Maintaining Relationships: The Core Principle

"Build a relationship with people with whom you do serious business. One can escape a deal but not a relationship easily."
—**SUNITA BIDDU**

Once you've established rapport with a prospect or client, your job is to stay in communication with that person, keep listening to their needs and issues as they arise, and—perhaps most importantly— keep them happy. That's why, once I've begun to work with a business contact, I shift gears to the next phase of my "attack," if you will: maintaining the relationship.

Why is this important? There are many reasons. One effect of maintaining a long-term sales relationship is the opportunity to upsell and cross-sell new products or upgrades. As I demonstrated above, you can also potentially increase your opportunities to sell to your clients if (1) they become a customer for life at a single company; (2) they move from Company A to Company B to Company C; or (3) you move from Company A to Company B, and so forth. In all of these cases, I've found that it's much easier to keep my business with one person going than to "prospect" all over again for a new client. Remember my example from **Chapter 2: F.A.C.E. the Day: Focus**—I may need to talk to a hundred prospects to get one sale. I'd much rather work with the customer I already have than pound the pavement all over again to find a new one.

Moreover, maintaining relationships results in more reciprocal connections with your clients. Research has shown that the best business-to-business (B2B) relationships emerge when the association operates more like a partnership. According to a study commissioned by Gallup called "Building Exceptional Business-to-Business Relationships," whether you're a Fortune 500 company or a small business, effective B2B relationships share the following common traits:

• **Risk-Taking.** Both sides are willing to take chances. For clients, this means making an investment in the relationship before a return is clear. For customers, this means being willing to spend more now for lower long-term costs and increased value down the line.

• **Transparency and Trust.** Salespeople know their customers' business and needs. Both sides are honest about their experience levels, costs, and margin requirements, and what they want to achieve. Joint objectives, goals, and expectations are shared. "Showing your cards" creates trust and allows both customers and suppliers to look for win/win opportunities.

• **Shared Vision.** Both the buyers and the sellers invest in new ideas, plan ahead, and take a long-term view. Both parties understand that any pay-off may not come this quarter or even this year.

Sales and client relations can become more informal, more personal, and more fun as the relationship grows. My primary technique in relationship maintenance (which I'll describe in more detail below) is to create an environment in which all of these qualities—risk-taking, transparency and trust, and shared vision—will thrive.

In a perfect world, some of your strongest sales relationships may even morph into friendships.

Maintaining Relationships: Putting the Principle into Play

> "The meeting of two personalities is like the contact of two chemical substances: if there is any reaction, both are transformed.
> **—CARL JUNG**

In many ways, the tactics in this chapter are similar to those I discussed in **Chapter 8: Establishing Rapport**. You still want to empower your client. You still want to ask questions, listen attentively, and get them talking. And you still want to express gratitude for the opportunity to do so. Only, now, they *are* your client. So you want to maintain contact with them and send gentle reminders: "Hey, I'm still out here. What do you need? How can I keep helping you?"

Here are the nine next logical steps once the door is open and you've established rapport:

1. Be Thankful. Send occasional unsolicited notes or emails thanking your client and letting them know that you appreciate the opportunity to serve them and monitor their well-being. You want to keep showing significant appreciation for their time, with appropriate messaging along the way, especially if they agree to go out with you after work (see below). (Please also see **Chapter 13: Phone; Chapter 14: Email;** and **Chapter 17: Handwritten Notes** for best practices on how to compose emails and notes.)

2. Assign Power. In any communication, make it clear that you'll never go over their head. They are in control. I often use terms like "your people," "your team," "your firm." They always decide the next steps, in partnership with you. You are at their service.

3. Begin Out-of-Office Activities. There's an old adage I use with my sales team: "Your very first meeting should always be in their office. Every meeting thereafter should involve a fork, a knife, or a glass." Getting your clients out of the office to an event changes the dynamic. Once I get my clients into a fancy restaurant, to a ball game, or onto the golf course, I'm in control. (*Shhh*. This is a secret. They don't know that.)

Traditionally, there are four types of client events: office meetings (sales presentations, demos); meals (lunches, dinners, drinks); entertainment and events (performances, sporting events, wine-tastings); and business and industry events (conferences, group meetings, "road shows"). To find out the kind of event a client is most comfortable at, ask probing questions about their past experiences: "What was the best corporate event or work-related event you ever attended?" The answer will tell you a lot about what might get them excited.

Some people are not comfortable going to dinner or an event with a business colleague because they're introverted, or dining in a fancy restaurant makes them nervous. It's not their style. Others may be allergic to social events like meals or entertainment because they don't want to be indebted to you, or they don't want to spend their precious after-work hours on business. Fortunately, there are many ways to lure out even the most reluctant client by cloaking entertainment as "education" or "networking." For other clients, after your initial in-office meetings and demos, you might begin with a meeting for coffee in a café. The next step might be lunch, then dinner, then a "fun" corporate event like a concert or performance. Of course, there are always those who, once they know you're footing the bill, jump in with two feet: "Great! Give me the wine list."

"Treat your business relationships like friendships (or potential friendships). Formality puts up walls, and walls don't foster good business
relationships. No one is loyal to a wall…except the one in China."
—STEVE PAVLINA

There is always a balancing act between entertaining the grateful and being taken advantage of by the greedy. Over the course
of your career, you will certainly encounter both. I've always really
enjoyed the grateful folks and felt bad for the greedy ones. It can
be either slightly humorous or very offensive to spend an evening
with someone who feels they're "getting one over on you."

Brief story: New York City's Le Cirque was one of the most
famous restaurants in the world back in its heyday. One time I
brought a new client there and handed him the wine list. It was a
rookie mistake: he ordered a $2,000 bottle. When we finished that,
he ordered another one. Back in Chicago, I had to pass in a $6,000
dinner receipt on my expense report. My sales manager kindly ate
the expense and allowed it to be a pricey lesson, and this particular
client ended up being well worth the investment.

Managing these situations is all part of the control dynamic. In
this case, the guy clearly wanted to be in control, call the shots, and
show off—all to make me squirm. Of course you don't want to be
taken advantage of, but some punches you can take with a smile.
You have to find the mix of servitude and hosting that best matches
your own personality and goals.

Sometimes you'll take one for the team, for the greater good.
Remember, if somebody is a greedy cad, it's really their loss in the end.

4. Get Business Out of the Way Early. Now that you've got your
client out of the office, you want to move from business-friendly
to trusted-friendship-friendly. Either avoid all business talk or

dispense with it quickly. An effective early conversation at the dinner table might be a simple "tie-down" to ensure that you've addressed their concerns; then you can pivot to more personal topics. Here's how you might deal quickly with the business talk:

• "I hope you enjoyed the demo of our product, Marla. So we can get this out of the way before we order our cocktails, tell me, how are we doing here? Is everything copacetic?"

• "Have you seen everything you need from us at this point, Ms. Chen? Do you have any questions or want to open any issues with us?"

• "Sofía, is there anybody else we should talk to on your team to get the job done?"

Once you've established that both of you are on the same page and reading the same story, move on. Getting that confirmation out of the way *before* you've begun your coffee, lunch, or evening brings people's defenses down and lets you begin developing a more personal relationship.

5. Get Personal. Speaking about things other than your business dealings is the secret recipe to forging a more informal, more personal, and more trustworthy relationship. You should be the one to initiate discussions of topics beyond business; your client may not feel able to take the plunge.

Easy starter topics include family, travel, hobbies, and sports. Here's a list of friendly discussion-starting questions:

• "Any vacations planned?"

• "Do you have kids?"

• "Where did you go to school?"

• "Did you go to XYZ conference?"

• "Have you always lived in the city?"

- "What's your favorite restaurant?"

- "Are you a sports fan?"

Any advance intel that you've obtained from your due diligence (see **Chapter 7**) is obviously going to come in handy here. Keep the tone light and friendly. Ask questions, show interest, and by all means don't monologue about your own life. You're here to draw them out.

When you're interacting with a client in a more casual social setting, it's important to be gregarious, friendly, and fun-loving. It's also important to keep your sense of humor. There's no better way to do this than by making fun of yourself. Share a self-deprecating or embarrassing story (not too off-color, please) or be the butt of your own joke, and you'll quickly ingratiate yourself with your client.

6. Kill with Kindness. I've seen a hundred different techniques for killing people with kindness, and most of them I've learned from the master, my former partner and friend Tom Newton. I'm a huge fan of ingratiating myself with business contacts and colleagues in order to get into a position of trust. I know it works too.

Kindness and appreciation can be shown in a number of ways. You might send swag that's practical, cool, entertaining, or cute. In the past Tom has been known to ask a client, "Does your family ever eat snacks while watching Netflix?" and then follow up with a box of popcorn, candy, or cookies. Tom might also send a basket full of candy bars, Red Bull, Monster energy drinks, and five-hour ENERGY shots, with a note saying, "This is to help get your energy up to sign the paperwork." As long as you think you can pull off your sense of humor, go for it. It usually works like a charm, and your clients will get a laugh. I've sent a giant FedEx box of t-shirts, golf balls, or pens to a client's office, so that it will feel like Christmas morning when they open it. Sending small gifts also provides a reason for you to follow up with them: "Hi, we just sent out some tins of pop-corn with our company logo. Did you get them?"

One of my favorite techniques for showing appreciation is another tactic I stole from Tom. He used to call clients and say, "We have a tradition at our company once a new account is open [or: whenever a client makes their first purchase with us]. We'd love to send over breakfast for your entire organization. What's better for your team, breakfast on a Monday or on a Friday? How many people? Do you have a favorite breakfast place?" That's not only a great thank you gift, but you can also use it as a bagel-on-a-stick incentive to close the sale. Asking, "When can we send over breakfast?" shifts the con-versation in your client's head away from "Are we going to sign on the dotted line?" to "When are we going to have this amazing free breakfast?" It also exemplifies the time-honored, classic approach of "speaking beyond the close"—seeing the end sale as part of a much longer implementation process, requiring continual care and "feed-ing" that goes well beyond the day the client chooses to sign.

Providing breakfast to an entire office or organization, beyond just the decision-maker, goes a long way toward building rap-port among the larger team and making them feel appreciated. Remember, these individuals are probably on a long-term career path within their industry, and they will hopefully remember you or your gesture down the line.

7. Involve Family and Friends. Conventional wisdom often says, "Don't invite the client's spouse or kids, or other clients, to a corpo-rate entertainment event for a newbie client." But, in my experience, doing so can actually be a secret weapon in relationship maintenance.

Asking your client to invite either their spouse or friends who aren't from the industry can create a comfortable atmosphere. With family and friends present at a restaurant, the event will feel more like a dinner party and less like a shakedown or bloodletting. By saying, "Bring your spouse! Bring your friends!" you're signaling, "This is going to be fun." The event is supposed to be informal, low-key, and low-stress because you want to bring your client closer to you personally.

Events like these are also another way to kill with kindness and let clients do something they might not otherwise be able to afford: "We have great seats for the Atlanta Braves. I know what it costs to take a family of four to a baseball game. I'd love it if you wanted to bring your wife and kids." Or "Bring a few of your friends. You'll have a sky box to yourself and a bar area where you guys get anything you need." I've held wine-tastings followed by the theater, as well as steak dinners followed by improv-comedy shows. The clients and spouses met great people, laughed their asses off, and weren't sold a damn thing all night long. Years later, attendees of one of these evenings commented that it was the coolest corporate event they'd ever been to—the best "corporate date night" ever.

Here's another reason to host these events: they give you an opportunity to assign your clients or prospects power and to treat them like gods in front of their spouses, kids, or peers. Say I run around and get my client, Mrs. Johnson, and her family drinks and hot dogs—that's going to make Mrs. Johnson seem like a big-shot and a decision-maker. Waiting on her and her family shows that I respect her position and that I will hustle to earn her business. It makes her feel good, and it's also going to impress Mr. Johnson.

8. Involve Business Associates. A business event can be a "big table," so you want to control who's at it. Another signature move that I learned from Tom and JJ is to invite other clients, from different companies, to sit at the table too. If you can surround your clients with other colleagues of yours, it's a huge win. Assuming that your relationships with these other, long-standing clients are solid (otherwise, why would you invite them?), they're going to say complimentary things about you and do part of the persuasion job for you. They'll make nice, pass on positive stories from other events you've hosted, and, along the way, subtly talk you up. In other words, good clients will do the selling for you.

New clients will also admire and envy the relationships you have with other business associates, wonder how you got to be friends with them, and feel grateful that now you're letting them into your circle of trust. "Wow, how the hell did Ed get to be buddies with Brett Taylor, president of Coca-Cola Financial?" Well, funny story: because Ed has cultivated a relationship with Brett, who used to be the treasurer, now Brett will come to dinner simply because he and his wife are Ed's friends. And Brett will say nice things about Ed. He might even give a toast and say, "Ed's a great guy to do business with." If you can surround your prospects with other clients of yours, your rapport with them will demonstrate what a future relationship with your potential new client might look like.

And perhaps *you* can be Brett Taylor ten years from now.

9. Stay in Touch. Once you've wined and dined your client and begun to establish a relationship, make an effort to stay in touch. As the relationship develops and becomes more informal, it's okay to send more casual notes or emails about non-business topics. You might communicate about a common interest you've discovered in pop culture, music, or sports. Or you could share an appropriately funny GIF or meme, or send a relevant article. You might wish your client a happy birthday or follow up on a family topic that the client has shared with you: "I hope your mom is feeling better," or "I hope your daughter's audition went well." Keep it simple, but maintain steady contact.

(See more of these tips in **Chapter 16: Meals, Entertainment, and Events** and in the **Appendix: A Planning Guide for Business, Sales, and Industry Events**.)

Maintaining Relationships: Try This

"Remember that the most valuable antiques are dear old friends."
—H. JACKSON BROWN JR.

Here's a great networking and relationship-maintenance tool: ask yourself, "Who am I not thinking about right now?" This is an obvious play on the old line "Try thinking about something you're not thinking about right now." In my version, I suggest reaching out to one person a week, ideally someone you haven't been in touch with for a while. That person might be one of the following:

• An old friend

• A former classmate

• A former colleague

• A client or prospect

• An industry contact

Either give them a call or send an email or LinkedIn message (or use any other social media) that simply says:

"I was just thinking about you and wanted to reach out. I hope this message finds you well. All the best."

It's important for the message to have no angle, no request, and no need for reciprocity. This sort of message will create good will, keep you in touch, and possibly make somebody's day.

If you do this just once a week, you will reach 52 people a year and over 520 people in a decade. Those numbers alone bode well for your network and potential relationships. It's always nice to be thought of, and people generally appreciate a polite and thoughtful message. There's little to lose. And even if your message is clumsy, as Ralph Waldo Emerson once said, "It is one of the blessings of old friends that you can afford to be stupid with them."

Sometimes, as a result of your reaching out, one of these contacts will think of you for business, fun, or something else positive—a great outcome.

Maintaining Relationships: Don't Try This

"A growing relationship can only be nurtured by genuineness."
—LEO BUSCAGLIA

Avoid Talking Too Much Business in Social Settings. As I mentioned above, when sitting down to a meal, get the business out of the way early. You don't want a casual lunch to become another stuffy, white-tablecloth, portfolio-manager discussion, in which the client is being sold or spoken to, not spoken with. It's hard to enjoy food or a concert if you're being pitched.

Avoid Being a Drunken Fool. This might be a client, or it might be you. Sometimes, someone at an event with an open bar might enjoy themselves a little too much and get out over their skis. Tread lightly until you know your own and your client's response to booze. In some cases, you might want to put a box around alcohol. Be aware of whether or not your client is getting hammered, and make sure they get home safely.

Don't Get Hosed (Too Badly, Too Often). Some clients manipulate and take advantage of salespeople. They like nice stuff, and they'll happily take you for a ride and never do any business with you. Be aware of the leeches and chronic takers. But also take it in stride: you will have to kiss some toads, and sometimes it takes a few experiences before you realize that you're courting an amphibian, not Prince or Princess Charming.

CHAPTER 10

PRESENTATION SKILLS

EDibles: (Don't) Fire Your Loins: A Cautionary Tale

*"No audience ever complained about a presentation
or speech being too short."*

—STEPHEN KEAGUE

At the dawn of time—well, the dawn of my business career, back in the early 1990s—I worked for a Pittsburgh-based administrator and distributor of bank-proprietary money funds called Concord Financial. One day I headed out to make an important sales call. I was meeting a treasurer of a major pharmaceutical company and was determined to land her as a client.

Beginning my pitch, I said, "We have this fund from Chase Manhattan," then flipped to the next slide in my PowerPoint deck. "We have this fund from Chemical. We have this fund from Bank of America, and Boatman's Bank, and Citibank." I paused. "It's up to you."

Then I used a line I'd said a hundred times before: "Really, whatever fund fires your loins."

Now, usually this line got a huge chuckle. Anyone who heard it would appreciate the irony and absurdity of a money fund getting somebody excited and firing their loins.

But this time, no dice. No laughter. Dead silence. "Did you just say, 'Whatever fires my loins'?" said the treasurer. Clearly she was not amused, and was possibly offended.

I tried to recover. "Uh, sorry... Too much, perhaps?"

But it was too late. For the rest of the meeting, she shot daggers at me. I could feel the tension. All I could think was "I've got to get out of this conference room now because this meeting is OVER." From that moment until I left, my presentation was pure torture.

Finally I ended the meeting and escaped. I raced out to the parking lot and fired up my Motorola, one of those old two-pound, Gordon-Gecko-style cell phones that gave you a half-hour of talking time for every battery charge and sold for $4,000. I called Chris Klutch, my boss at the time. "Chris, I think you're going to get a phone call. I want you to hear it from me first, so you can decide what you want to do." Then I explained what had happened, expecting to get fired.

Chris listened to my recap, and, to his credit, he thought my implosion was the funniest thing he'd ever heard. "Don't let it get you down," he advised me. "Move on to the next client. It's a funny line, and she can't take a joke."

But that early blunder has haunted me. I'm telling you this cautionary tale, this war story from my early years, because it's an example of how, when making a presentation, a salesperson can step over the line. I had veered from "professional" and "friendly" to "inappropriate banter" too quickly. And I've never lived it down.

Now, looking back, I can see it as a funny story. (In the intervening years, I hope that treasurer has had a change of heart too.) Recently I asked my colleague JJ to tell me his favorite sales quote. He said, "My favorite sales line of all time is 'Does that fire your loins?'"

Hysterical. Thanks a lot, JJ.

Presentation Skills: The Core Principle

"Don't over-sell it, or you could end up buying it back."
—JEFF "JJ" JELLISON, CO-FOUNDER
AND MANAGING DIRECTOR, ICD

Over my career, if you add it all up, I've given approximately five thousand sales presentations. There are multiple ways that a presentation can go wrong or just not be memorable. You name it, and I've seen the wipe-out.

I've seen technology go wrong. I've been at Google for a presentation only to realize that I couldn't get on the internet. (I tried googling my problem, but that didn't work...) I've given a presentation at Hewlett-Packard only to be told, "Good presentation. We just wish you hadn't done it on a Dell computer." Oops.

I've seen the wrong people in the room. I've seen the wrong materials come up on the screen. I've seen reps walk in with me and have no materials—no brochures, no PowerPoint deck, nothing. Some salespeople are cavalier and fly by the seat of their pants. They'll say to me, "We're just going to go and have a chat." I reply, "Uh, no. We're not."

I've also seen over-prepared. One sales rep who worked for me was famous for going into a meeting with a hundred-slide deck. It was like flipping through *War and Peace*. Just skip to the end: does anybody live? I've been in presentations that have meandered so far off topic that they had nothing to do with why anyone was in the room. I've been in presentations where clearly the salesperson (okay, me) hadn't properly prepared the client for the discussion, and I've gone into a conference room and realized that mainly I was just there to hear myself talk. A lot of salespeople, especially early in their careers, talk too much about their product, not about what the customer needs.

As a salesperson, you learn how to block these failures from your memory. You have to keep moving forward. But you should learn something from every wipe-out. You can't be afraid of failure because, as another sales adage goes, "Every loss puts you that much closer to the win." If you're committed to the numbers game, even after you get egg on your face, say to yourself, "Well, I've got only nine more sales calls to go before somebody's going to say yes."

My point is that mastering the art of giving a powerful presentation is a key skill for any salesperson. And when it comes to presentation skills, you can't practice, or "sharpen your ax," too often.

Presentation Skills: Putting the Principle into Play

"Successful presentations are understandable,
memorable, and emotional."
—CARMINE GALLO

The Five Tactical Presentation Skills

These are the five pillars—or what I call "tactical skills"—of giving effective and professional sales presentations:

1. Setting the Stage. Button down all the details in advance, and be prepared for any possible problem.

2. Clarity of Message. Explain the purpose and outline a road-map for the meeting.

3. Active Listening. Pay attention to your prospect's reactions in real time.

4. Effective Tie-Downs. Get buy-ins at various junctures to lead your prospect toward your product.

5. Call to Action. Propose next steps to keep the deal moving forward.

Now here are the details of each of these five pillars, with suggestions for how to put them into practice in your presentations:

1. Setting the Stage

"Pretend that every single person you meet has a sign around his or her neck that says, 'Make me feel important.' Not only will you succeed in sales, you will succeed in life."
—MARY KAY ASH

Due Diligence. This topic is so important that I've devoted an entire chapter to it in this book (see **Chapter 7**). But due diligence is also part of setting the stage before your first presentation. Check again that you've researched your prospect thoroughly, and make sure that what you're selling meets your prospect's needs.

Professional Presentation Preparation. You're aiming for an A-plus presentation—one where you walk in, the technology is tight, and both you and your materials are ready. The prospect should walk in, see a good show, and leave with all their questions answered. That's an A-plus. But, just like in school, you need to put in some preparation to get that high grade. Here's a checklist of questions that will help you make sure that you've prepared enough for your meeting, before you enter the room:

• **Do You Have All Your Materials?** Do you have a computer, and the right deck of slides loaded onto that computer? Do you also have printed copies of your deck as a backup? (See "Do you have backups?" below.) Have you previewed and triple-checked your deck? Your prospect may ask for a copy in advance, which is usually a good sign. If your presentation includes a demonstration of a product, is that ready to go (and customized for your client)?

• **Have You Confirmed the Agenda and Your Available Time?** Be clear about your goals for the meeting: "We're going to give you a little history on the company. We're going to give you a quick demo. We're going to answer any questions you have." Confirm with the prospect what you'll be talking about and who will be present, including their names and titles. Make sure that your presentation is customized to the length of the time you've been given. Call ahead and test the waters: "We'll probably need thirty minutes, maybe a little more. It'd be great if you could give us an hour. Is that possible?" Most customers will set their own time-frame. Personally, I usually ask for an hour and plan for an hour and a half, to have adequate time before and after the meeting. Then be flexible. I've had meetings go on for two and a half hours because the prospect was clearly intrigued and asked to extend the time. Don't flinch for a second. The correct answer is "Sure, I can go late. I'll grab another flight tomorrow morning."

• **Have You Confirmed the Room Set-Up?** Find out if you can get into the conference room or meeting space at least fifteen minutes ahead of time to stake out the room; set up your equipment; test the technology, such as the projector, screen, and internet connection; and confirm what you need to have, such as cables or adapters. You don't want to deal with last-minute snafus or run around troubleshooting right before your presentation, or you might end up doing hand-shadow puppets and flipping through a lame paper deck. Room set-up can be the difference between an A-plus presentation and a C-minus.

• **Do You Have Backups?** There are many reasons to make sure that you have digital, cloud, and paper backups of all your materials: technology malfunctions, loss or theft, or simply forgetting to bring what you need. When in doubt, good old-fashioned paper will do the trick. Numerous redundancies can't hurt.

2. Clarity of Message

"I hate the way people use slide presentations instead of thinking. People would confront a problem by creating a presentation. I wanted them to engage, to hash things out at the table, rather than show a bunch of slides. People who know what they're talking about don't need PowerPoint."

—STEVE JOBS

"Why Are We Here Today?" Begin with introductions and a preview of the meeting. This is a chance to get to know everyone in the room, get their okay for your game plan (time, agenda, content), and show appreciation. "Angelica, we appreciate your time. Why are we here today? We're excited to show you our new product. Before we go any further, let me make sure we're presenting on what you need. Do I have this correct?" Tie down and confirm. Even if they throw you a curveball—"Uh, actually, what we had in mind was…"—it's better to know that before you begin and not half an hour into your PowerPoint. Pivot and say, "Okay, that sounds great, though it's not what we prepared for. Today we're ready to talk to you about numbers one, two, and three. Number four we'd like to show you in a demo that we can do online remotely, whenever you guys are available. Can we schedule that?" Live to fight another day.

The Three "Tells." As Winston Churchill once said, "If you have an important point to make, don't try to be subtle or clever. Use a pile driver. Hit the point once. Then come back and hit it again. Then hit it a third time—a tremendous whack."

There's an old business-school adage:

1. Tell them what you're about to tell them.

2. Tell them.

3. Then tell them what you just told them.

In your presentation, give a preview first; then present; then wrap up with a summary at the end.

Identify Problems, Then Provide Solutions. Traditionally, when I say, "Why are we here today?" it's in order to identify a prospect's problems. Some examples from my world of fintech: "I see you've got an arcane, DOS-based bank system that requires a crank to start and doesn't disclose who you are as an investor to the fund." Or "I see you're in a non-disclosed environment, so you're not getting relationship credit with the vendors you're using." Or "I remember you saying that you're not getting any data flow into your treasury workstation because it's not linked to the product you're using today. You've got no synchronicity." Or "I see your fund selection is really limited because you're using this bank-proprietary product that only lets you buy JP Morgan, JP Morgan, or JP Morgan."

Then pivot to your solution—you're here to save the day: "Well, we'd like to show you something today that could address all of those issues." Framing your presentation as a solution to a specific problem is another way of reminding them:

1. Why you're meeting

2. That you understand their concerns and are going to address them with your product

3. That your product can save them time, money, or both—that it's either more effective or more efficient than their current process

Provide Examples of Clients with Similar Concerns. How you address this depends on your business and the community with which your prospect identifies. It never hurts to use household names as examples or, as previously discussed, local references that will assure them they're not alone in choosing your product or solution. Your goal with these comparisons is to show that your product has solved similar issues for other companies.

3. Active Listening

"Listening is an art that requires attention over talent,
spirit over ego, others over self."
—DEAN JACKSON

Many salespeople think of a presentation as "Me, me, me." But, in reality, any *good* presentation isn't about you, it's about your prospect: "Them, them, them." That's why effective, active listening is such a critical presentation skill—one that is often overlooked in the art of giving a good presentation. It's also another way to flex your business-etiquette muscles.

Some younger, overly enthusiastic types are so over-prepared that they're laser-focused on getting through the content of their presentation. They keep their heads down, reading from their screen or their notes. Old-timers can be guilty of the same mistake.

Arrogant, oblivious types drone on about themselves without being present or caring about what's happening around them.

Presenters need to ask themselves constantly, "Is my audience engaged? If not, how can I engage them before I lose them?" Active listening can help, and here are some strategies for achieving it:

- **Focus on the Prospect, Not Yourself.**
  - Have their biggest issues on the page in front of you.
  - Keep track of whether or not you've addressed them, and check them off as you go.
  - Ask good qualifying questions.
- **Tune into the Prospect's Concerns.**
  - Show empathy and understanding of their job description.
  - Remind them of what problem you're there to solve.
- **Show Them You're Paying Attention.**
  - Take detailed notes during the meeting. This is a respectful and effective tool to show that you're engaged and interested.
  - Engage in eye contact, affirmations, and positive body language.

Active listening is such an important topic that this book designates a whole chapter to it. Read more in **Chapter 12: Active Listening.**

4. Effective Tie-Downs

> "Don't find customers for your products,
> find products for your customers."
> —SETH GODIN

What Are Tie-Downs? How do you know when you're close to your prospect saying yes? In the context of an effective sales presentation, you can use certain phrases at key decision points to lead your customer down a logical path that ends at your product. These are called tie-downs. Throughout your sales process, you should tie down your client as often as you can.

Effective tie-downs are an art in professional sales. The concept is this: Get a customer's buy-in, confirmation, and commitment along the way. Lead the customer through checkpoints—mileposts along the way to your conclusion, which is your client driving away in that shiny new car. The further down the road they go, the harder it will be for them to turn back. When customers start nodding at your tie-downs, they're close to the close.

Always Be Closing (ABC). "Tying down" is a polite way of saying "closing." But nobody likes to be closed on, right?

This is Sales 101, and for a lot of people techniques like the "if/then" close or the "alternative" close, evoking images of a used-car salesman wearing white patent-leather shoes and polyester pants, make them nauseous. You know the shtick: "Ma'am, what's it going to take to get you into this car today?" Ick. In your tie-downs, you want to avoid that image, but unfortunately—and fortunately—these principles *do* work, because they effectively lead people down the logical path to your product. Done more subtly, they can work for you.

In your sales presentations, always move toward the close by building in tie-ins as you go. Let's take a look at two classic closes: the "if/then" close and the "alternative" close.

• **The "If/Then" Close.** Whether you know it or not, you've probably experienced this one (or been a victim of it). "Ms. Banerjee, *if* we can show you an insurance policy today that makes sense for you financially, that will provide the coverage you need, and that you can afford, *then* are you prepared to proceed?" But beware: this close has to be subtle and polite, or it can reek of that sleazy used-car salesguy.

The idea is "If we can do 1, 2, 3, then are you ready to go?" If/then. The logic of this argument is airtight. For example, "Okay, we've discussed what's important to you, and what's important to you is (1) ease of use for the system, (2) safety of principle, (3) liquidity, and (4) improved integration and reporting. Assuming we show all four of these things to your satisfaction, when are you looking to move forward?" This example uses the "if/then" close, but in a less obtrusive way. If we can show you everything to your satisfaction, everything that matches your criteria, then what's your timeline? Try to identify their next logical step.

• **The Alternative Close.** Here's how this one works: "It's been a great pleasure presenting to you today. I'm really glad you enjoyed our conversation. Would it be better to get started on Wednesday or Thursday of next week?" You're not asking a prospect whether or not they want to get started. You're giving them a choice, an alternative, that does not allow them to say no. In car-sales speak, "Do you want the car in red or in blue?" not "Do you want the car?"

There are effective and polite ways to be always closing without being too pushy. Some techniques are matters of personal choice, and a lot of them are situational. Always be leading the client down the logical path that ends at your product.

Use Confirmations. Confirmations are unobtrusive ways to move your client toward a sale. Each yes makes the next affirmation a little bit easier. If you get people on the "path of yes," so that they're nodding and feeling happy, then they'll feel at ease and be more likely to want to buy your product. Here are some confirmations that I've used throughout my career, all of which help get a prospect closer to "Yes":

- **"Do you agree?"** Insert an easy-to-agree-with idea here. "I like cold beer. Do you agree?" The probable response is "Yes, I do prefer my beer cold." Who wouldn't agree to that? Yes, that's okay. Yes, that's a good thing. Yes, I like oxygen.

- **"Are we on the same page?"** Use this to confirm agreement. "We understand you'd like to have this conversion completed by the end of the year. Are we on the same page?"

- **"Does this make sense?"** This is another pleasant way of confirming that you both see the issue from the same point of view. You understand each other. "So that's the end of our presentation. Does it all make sense?" I use this one often, and I'm made fun of for it. But I use it throughout my day because it works.

Tie-downs, closes, and confirmations are necessary checkpoints along the road to the close, moments when you pause your presentation to ask:

- "How are we doing?"
- "How's everybody holding up?"
- "Are you seeing this?"
- "Are you feeling this?"
- "Are you liking this?"

If they aren't with you, adjust.

An effective presenter keeps tabs on the situation in the room. Has anyone in the meeting drifted away? Have you lost someone? Are they staring at their phone? If a big decision-maker walks into a room and plops their phone down on the table, you'll know you're in for a challenge to hold their attention. For some, having their phone at the ready is an escape mechanism. For others, the phone might send another signal: "Check out how important I am. I need my mobile in case the White House calls me."

Tie-downs not only help to ensure that you're holding everyone's attention, they're a way to show that it's a two-way conversation. They're also a great way to help the customer come to grips with the decision to buy your product, reaffirming along the way that you're delivering what they need.

Summarize Your Product's Attributes Versus Competitors. When I make a presentation, I'm not there to knock or attack a competitor, or "unsell" anybody else. But I might say this to a prospect: "We're operating under the assumption that you're not satisfied with your current provider, or we wouldn't be in this room, right? Can you tell me what your least favorite things are about the system/product/solution you have right now?" As you go, try to address those issues in your demonstration, and offer a tie-down: "Can you see how this reporting system would be a significant improvement for your risk-management team?" By asking questions like this one you're providing a mental laundry list for your prospect of why your product, compared with the product they're currently using, is a better solution.

5. Call to Action

"Do you want to know who you are? Don't ask. Act!
Action will delineate and define you."
—THOMAS JEFFERSON

You're in the conference room, and the presentation is almost over. "We've shown you the system," you say. "It's user-friendly. We've shown that it's at no cost to you. You agree with those facts. Is there anything we're missing?" Or "Would this system improve your current situation?"

Then you have to be quiet. Once you've asked for a closing decision, you've got to shut your mouth. That awkward silence is the only real pressure that salespeople ever get to apply to prospects. Be silent.

If the prospect's answer is yes—as in, "Yes, we'll buy" or "Yes, we're interested but we need to..." or even "Maybe," then you've arrived at the last component of a professional tactical presentation: the call to action. Here are some key steps to get them to say yes:

Develop a Road-Map to Get Started. Ask your client to tell you about their process. You might say, "Now that you've found the right system, how will you go about making a change? Help us outline what the next steps are, because we want to be respectful of your process. We don't want to push or bother anybody. But we do want to stay in front of you. Can you tell us what the road-map [or "timeline," "implementation plan," "strategy"] looks like from here?"

This road-map might include paperwork and implementation timelines. It might mean that you provide them with account-opening documents or references. It might mean that a contract needs to be sent to their legal department and vetted. Sending paperwork and setting implementation timelines are the preferred outcomes. That's the door you most want to go through. You might say, "Great, I'm really glad you like the system. Who from your team reviews this kind of paperwork? What sort of timeline suits you and your team for this implementation?" Then, again, shut up.

Help the Prospect Outline the Needed "Next Step" Action Items. Here's where you say, "What we'd love to do now is outline the next steps or action items from here. What do you need from us?" The potential client may say, "Thanks, we don't need anything at this point. Let us think about it." That's okay. In this situation, to regain control of the sale, you might say, "So we all agree that we've shown you a better system, right? Great. How about we send you the paperwork for your review—no pressure. Is that a good place to start?"

Another prospect might reply, "You know what, we're working on six other projects right now. We're not going to get to this until Q1." Your "next step" action item here is to keep the relationship alive. You might say, "We want to earn your business. If you were me, what would you do between now and Q1? We don't want to be a pest, but we'd really like to help you make this as painless as possible. What if we could pre-populate all the paperwork for you and offer an incentive for getting started earlier?" There might be other incentives you can offer for an earlier kick off, such as a discount. Or you might run a tally of the opportunity cost of not changing to your product.

If the prospect says they're still undecided, you can work another angle. "Great. I'm going to be back in Chicago in February, because the weather's so beautiful here in February. Maybe we could grab lunch or dinner when I'm back in town?" In other words, bluff. Or "You know, I'm going to be back in Snowball, Minnesota, because I'm hosting a client event in mid-February, and it'd be a great opportunity for you to meet some of the other local treasurers and ask them what their experience with us has been." This provides an additional call to action and next step. If they say yes...then scramble to set up that trip to Chicago or that dinner in Snowball, Minn.

Put the Call to Action on the Final Slide. Sometimes, after a successful presentation, when the prospect has said all the right things and they'd like to get started, you'll be eager to get out of there. You'll push the paperwork across the desk, call a Lyft, and head to the airport.

Not so fast. A clear call to action is a powerful way to wrap up a well-thought-out presentation. It can be a clincher to put "Next steps?"—with an outlined call to action—right there on the final slide or page of your PowerPoint, or on printed collateral. Something like:

- *We* need to send you paperwork.

- *We* need to come back in two weeks to run a demo.

- *You* need to fill out the paperwork.

- *You* need to send a list of who gets the demo.

Summarize Your Presentation by Telling Prospects What You Just Told Them. End your presentation with a clear summary: "Here's what we discussed today. Did we address the issues you were concerned about? Here are the points we have tried to address. Were these clearly covered?" Tell them what you told them. It's another kind of tie-down.

Speak Past the Deal. As we've seen, "speaking past the deal" is a call-to-action strategy that you can use at different stages of the sales process. If you're afforded a window of opportunity by the customer, if they're nodding and saying, "Yes, we could really use this product," get them to see past the immediate deal. Say, "Hey, when you guys are on board, we'll invite you to a fun users' event that we do in San Francisco every spring." Or "We are so grateful for this opportunity and can't wait to get started." Another effective example of speaking past the deal is the "When do you want breakfast?" close mentioned in **Chapter 9: Maintaining Relationships**.

This is a nuanced technique, so use it only when things are going well. If you can make "speaking past the deal" a natural and fluid part of your conversation, you'll put the client at ease. By speaking as if the transaction is already in the can, you'll lower the buyer's anxiety and make them feel, since the decision has already been made, that they don't have a big, scary choice to make.

Also, by referring to the prospect as a client and referencing all the great benefits they're going to receive as a client, the prospect will start seeing themselves as that client. "You're gonna love it when..."

Show Appreciation, Sincerity, and Confidence. This goes without saying, but having the full attention of a single person or a whole team is a big deal. You need to show your thanks for their time and participation, and for hosting you. As I discussed in **Chapter 8: Establishing Rapport**, it's crucial to remember that polite and professional communication always harks back to the cornerstones of good manners and etiquette—"please" and "thank you." Express gratitude for the opportunity to meet the prospect, and follow up with an appropriate email or handwritten note.

I think it's also appropriate to say, "You won't regret going with us," or "We won't let you down. If you have any concerns, please speak to a few of our existing customers to hear about their experience of doing business with us." Statements like these can build confidence and are a great way to end a presentation or meeting.

Pandemic Protocols:
Presentation Skills in the Age of the Coronavirus

"It has become appallingly obvious that our technology has exceeded our humanity." —**Albert Einstein**

Here's the big $64,000 question. Wait, update that figure to the $64 million question: How will the pandemic and the looming threat of future infectious diseases affect how salespeople get their jobs done, especially when it comes to sales presentations?

Maybe it's too early to tell. For some, it has already meant the death of a salesman. Some industries are pressing pause, or punting, or waiting on making deals until sales calls can be made in person again. In other cases, business has accelerated.

Sales teams are using Zoom and other video-conferencing tools, investing in training, and migrating their sales techniques to online forums. As you know, giving a presentation to a prospect means a lot more than rolling through a PowerPoint slide deck. Presenting involves a demonstration of the product as well. In my area of business, called SaaS, or "Software as a Service," almost all the deals have some form of remote demonstration. Clearly these can and should continue remotely. Usually, also, people are amenable to accepting a demo online because it's low-pressure and you can customize the demo to their needs.

For other industries, remotely "demo-ing" the product—a new car, for instance—presents challenges. Most people want to touch the car, sit in it, and drive it before signing on the dotted line. Salespeople are already harnessing tools like FaceTime to give live tours of cars and show particular features. That said, perhaps a positive outcome of the pandemic is that people are less fearful of buying products remotely, sight unseen. Also, many salespeople are already accustomed to working remotely, from their homes or cars or hotel rooms, so the transition to out-of-office sales shouldn't feel like heavy lifting.

Here are some ways to adapt your prospecting and presentation techniques during the pandemic:

• **Focus on Existing Clients.** Instead of finding new customers, now is the time to give your existing clients extra attention and love, and concentrate on meeting their needs.

• **Harness Video Content.** Use canned videos or live-streaming to demonstrate your products or give tours of your facilities. Keep your clients informed with video blogs, tutorials, and webinars. Use recorded customer testimonials and interviews to promote your services. Take advantage of remote capabilities by including team-members not normally present. Be creative.

• **Be Tech Savvy.** During video conferencing, dress professionally, find a quiet, neutral space in your home (or home office), and make sure you have a good wifi signal, adequate lighting, and a high-quality camera and headset for clear audio and video. Use the video-conferencing platform of your choice to connect with clients. Zoom is popular, but Cisco Webex Meetings, Citrix GoToMeeting, Microsoft Teams, and Jitsi Meet are also well-regarded. Screen-sharing, annotation tools, and whiteboarding are useful features. Use video conferencing sparingly to prevent burn-out.

• **Be Empathetic, Pitch Differently.** Aim for high-quality engagement with your prospect or client. Listen and be sensitive. Now is the time to support clients who need help adjusting to the pandemic. Alter your offerings and/or sales pitch to address "pain points" raised by the pandemic. Don't prey on them in a vulnerable time; instead reposition your product or service as a solution to these new issues.

• **Educate, Adapt, and Keep Going**. Continue checking in with your prospects, keep your connections alive, and keep the conversation open. Things can change fast, so stay alert and be ready to pivot.

CHAPTER 11

TRANSFER OF ENTHUSIASM

EDibles: A Pivotal Turning Point

"If you're going to do something, do it with energy. Don't go through the motions. If you're going to commit to something, go hard. Half steps rarely pay dividends."

—RUSS DRIVER, FORMER DIRECTOR OF DEUTSCHE ASSET MANAGEMENT

I grew up in Sacramento, California. I had attended only private parochial schools until I enrolled at San Diego State University. I moved to campus in freshman year with my Jesuit education, thinking, "I'm a pretty bright kid. I know my stuff. I'm going to kill this."

Suddenly I found myself in a school of forty-five thousand students. Nobody was watching me. No one cared whether I went to class or not. Nobody was going to call my mom if I didn't turn in a paper.

I totally tanked my first semester. I believe I clocked a resounding 1.7 GPA. I had also been rowing crew, and my bad grades put my rowing in jeopardy. That was a severe wake-up call for me. I was put on academic probation. I needed to shape up or, quite literally, I would be shipped out.

At the time I loved English and writing, and I intended to major in Journalism. I thought that being a reporter or lobbyist was the career path for me. But when I returned for my second semester, an impactful teacher changed my path. Her name was Dr. Shirley Weber.

I had to take a class called Speech 103, a general education requirement for my major. The class was over-enrolled, but luckily there was an equivalent class, Speech 104, that would satisfy the same requirement. Dr. Weber taught Speech 104, in what San Diego State now calls the Department of Africana Studies. Preference was given to those majoring in African-American studies, but I showed up on the first day of class anyway, figuring they might have space.

Essentially, I crashed the first day of class. I was the only white face in the room. Afterward I approached Dr. Weber. "Is there room in the class?" I asked, more than a little intimidated.

"Maybe you don't understand that there's a priority here for African-American students," Dr. Weber said.

"Well," I replied, "is there room?"

"Yeah, there's room in the class."

"So are you saying I can't take the class?"

Dr. Weber looked me in the eye. "All right," she said, laughing. "Okay, then, smarty-pants. Give it a try."

I gave it a try, and I crushed it. It became one of my favorite classes. I remember vividly each of the different speeches that I gave that semester. One of my best-received topics was hangovers and the best ways to avoid them, other than sobriety.

Some powerful lessons came out of that experience. One was that I got my first A+ for a college class, which began to pull my GPA out of its nosedive and gave me confidence. I was also able to repurpose the material from my speeches in my stand-up comedy.

The other lesson is that Dr. Weber challenged me to rethink my future path. Toward the end of the term, she pulled me aside and said, "What's your major?"

I told her Journalism.

"You should really consider switching to Speech Communications.

You've got a gift, and you'd be crazy not to look at it."

When a teacher you admire says something that powerful, especially to a desperate eighteen-year-old, you'd be crazy not to move on it. That afternoon, I changed my major. As a result of studying Speech Communications, I also became a student of the Civil Rights Movement and a follower of Dr. King. That small decision to take Speech 104 became one of the most pivotal turning points of my life.

Years later, my mother told me that I went to college as one person and came back a totally different guy, with new values and a new perspective. Getting involved in the Speech Department opened my eyes to the world of public speaking. What followed was my first foray into stand-up comedy, theater, music, and becoming somebody who enjoys making people laugh. Which eventually led me into sales, and what I call "corporate stand-up" today.

All of this was due to the influence of Dr. Weber. She managed to transfer her enthusiasm about what I couldn't see—my future—to me, a young, impressionable college student. In other words, her passion drove me to action.

As for Dr. Weber, she taught at San Diego State for forty years, chaired the Department of Africana Studies, and became president of the National Council for Black Studies. She also served as president of the San Diego Board of Education and chairwoman of the San Diego Citizens' Equal Opportunity Commission. Today she's a politician serving in the California State Assembly, where she sits on the Assembly's Committee on Higher Education. A distinguished career if ever there was one.

Thank you, Dr. Weber.

Transfer of Enthusiasm: The Core Principle

"Enthusiasm wins it all the time. While it may seem natural to wear
a long face sometimes and go under the weather on occasions,
experience has shown it is far better to be on the attack by constantly creating a momentum of energy, excitement, and passion."
—ABIODUN FIJABI

I've been a big fan of motivational speaker and sales guru Brian
Tracy for years. Back in the early days of my career, I attended one
of his sales seminars, then bought cassettes of his lectures, which
came in a plastic book. I'd listen to audiotapes of his business and
self-improvement talks in my Volkswagen Quantum wagon as I
drove around the Bay Area selling Minolta photocopiers. I listened
to those tapes on my way to work, during work, and after work,
until the magnetic tape turned to dust.

Suffice it to say, I'm a card-carrying member of the Brian Tracy
Fan Club. In his book *The Psychology of Selling: Increase Your Sales
Faster and Easier Than You Ever Thought Possible*, Tracy coined the
phrase "transfer of enthusiasm." He writes:

> The primary emotion in sales success is enthusiasm. Enthusiasm
> accounts for 50 percent or more of all sales ability. One of the
> very best definitions of a sale is "a transfer of enthusiasm."
>
> When you transfer your enthusiasm for your product or
> service into the mind and heart of your prospect, like an elec-
> trical connection, the sale takes place. When your emotional
> commitment and belief in the goodness of what you are selling
> transfers into the mind of the prospect or customer, all hesita-
> tion to buy disappears.
>
> Once again, there is a direct link between how much you like

yourself, your self-esteem, and your level of enthusiasm. The more you like yourself, the more enthusiastic you are. The more enthusiastic you are about your company and your product, the more enthusiastic the customer will become. Anything you do to raise your self-esteem will increase your ability to sell.

In this chapter, I give you my own take on Tracy's concept, adding my personal philosophy. Here goes.

My spin is that you have to be genuinely excited about your product and what it can do before somebody else will want to buy it from you. During your sales pitch, if you're mailing it in or BS-ing somebody, they will sense it like a dog senses fear. If you're not feeling it, don't fake it, because your efforts are not going to work.

If it's real, people will sense your enthusiasm. This principle is as much about your attitude while interacting with your prospects and clients as it is about how hard you sell to them.

You could also substitute the words "confidence" or "optimism" or "peace of mind" for "enthusiasm." If you're genuinely enthusiastic, it's confidence that people will sense when you walk into the room. It's optimism that people will feel as you extoll the features and benefits of your product or solution. It's peace of mind that people will experience as you answer their questions.

Transfer of enthusiasm is about cultivating feelings—tapping into how people feel and how excited they are. Make them feel how happy they could be to become part of something that feels like the right decision, something bigger than they are, something important, something enjoyable, maybe even something that's making a difference. If you can do that, you're effectively transferring enthusiasm from yourself to someone else. Bravo.

Enthusiasm can permeate many, if not all, facets of your life. The primary thrust of this book is about the power of good manners and etiquette. It's powerful to be enthusiastic about manners and etiquette, and to let that enthusiasm spill over to your business contacts. In doing so, you're not "sneaking one past the goalie." You're being proud of and deliberate with your manners. If you're genuine in your enthusiasm and politeness, there's no need to trick people.

Transfer of Enthusiasm: Putting the Principle into Play

"I began to realize how important it was to be an enthusiast in life. [My uncle] taught me that if you are interested in something, no matter what it is, go at it at full speed ahead. Embrace it with both arms, hug it, love it, and above all become passionate about it. Lukewarm is no good. Hot is no good either. White hot and passionate is the only thing to be."

—ROALD DAHL

The Top Techniques of Transferring Enthusiasm to Prospects, Clients, and Business Contacts

1. Be the Expert. During my years as Global Head of Sales at ICD, I could walk into any company at any level without hesitation, confident that I was among the world's premier experts on money fund and portal technology. Few, if any, people on the planet knew more about that technology, system, service, and delivery than I did. In the conference room, I fed off the energy this knowledge gave me. I'd think to myself, "There is no pitch I can't hit."

You too need to have that level of confidence in your knowledge. It's critically important to be well-versed in your field and feel confident that you have the best understanding of your product of anyone out there. But guess what? This knowledge doesn't come from reading the CliffsNotes in the car before arriving at a client meeting. Spend time on your homework, research the prospect, and stay on top of industry news and your competitors' moves. If you do, you can enter any meeting with confidence and enthusiasm.

Being the expert also means being organized and prepared. Rehearse and memorize verbal pitches for any situation, be it a conference, a trade show, or a coffee meeting. At a moment's notice, you should be able to deliver:

• A thirty-second hook

• A two-minute synopsis of your product or service

• Printed materials that you can walk through quickly and leave with a prospect or send later

• A demo of your product or service (or be able to schedule one for your prospect ASAP)

2. Be Positive. As I discussed in **Chapter 3: F.A.C.E. the Day: Attitude**, being positive is an important tool in a salesperson's toolbox. It's also key to transferring enthusiasm.

Imagine, if you will, that you and I are at a conference in your industry—healthcare, retail, finance, it doesn't matter. We're walking around a trade show together as customers. On our left is a booth that we'll call Option A. Three or four people sit there, staring at their phones, looking disinterested, never glancing up at the throngs passing by. They look tired, and they might be hungover. They've also got their suitcase next to them, as if they can't wait for the show to end. That's bad energy they're sending. Why would you and I go out of our way to talk to those zombies, or consider buying anything from them?

Now we walk on a bit farther and see a booth on the right, Option B. This booth is staffed by a group of well-dressed, smiling, laughing salespeople. They're making eye contact and engaging people who walk by. They've got energy and enthusiasm, and they've attracted a crowd. Naturally we gravitate toward them. We want to be someplace where something is going on. After chatting with them for a while, we say, "What are you guys doing later?"

Option B is much more appealing. And that's the mood you want to create when you walk into the room for a meeting or presentation. You want to project an authentic and genuine vibe and bring enjoyment to the table. Be positive, be engaging, and smile. Show appreciation for the time and opportunity to meet with your prospects.

Above all, be optimistic. Outcomes aren't guaranteed because you're an optimist, but optimism creates all the right conditions for good stuff to happen—and it can be contagious.

3. Express Pride. Exuding how much you love or enjoy working for your company is another way to make prospects feel enthusiastic about your product or service. Ideally this can be done with genuine and honest feeling. But if you do not, in fact, feel loyalty to your employer or what you're selling, how can you convey that sense? This can be a tough challenge because, at least in my industry, employees change business cards as often as I change my shorts. Loyalty ain't what it used to be.

Nevertheless, regardless of how long you've worked for your current employer, come up with a story, make sure it's tight, and be able to convey it in three quick sentences. Even if you're not "loving it," you need to deliver a persuasive answer. Some ideas:

• "Company X is a fantastic place to work because they put the clients first. We work for the customer."

• "Company X creates an entrepreneurial environment where we can contribute, bring ideas, and evolve quickly."

- "There's enormous opportunity for growth and expansion at Company X, so it's great for me and my family."

Any combination of these three ideas should resonate with your client. Ideally, your explanation won't be total BS; as long as there's some sincerity, your expression of enthusiasm will come across as believable.

It's great to be enthusiastic not only about your company but also about your team. You might say, "Fred, with this deal you'll get Tina here as your rep. Tina's got an excellent reputation with her clients, who are all over the country. They just love her, and she's a great person to have in your corner. You'll have her at your service for the entirety of your relationship with us. Also, Tina's income is predicated on your happiness." Comments like this help to strengthen the client's enthusiasm for the deal.

4. Tap into Archetypes and Emotions. To use this "transfer of enthusiasm" technique, you have to understand what ethos or archetypal role will motivate or inspire the prospect. What emotions can your client tap into by selecting your product or firm? To find out, appeal to your client's personality or company identity.

There are different narratives—stories, if you will, each with accompanying emotions—that your prospect might tap into to identify with your company, making them feel better about saying yes. You need to figure out what story will excite them and make them want to choose your product. (Remember, you can't use every one of these archetypes, because some won't logically apply to your company or product.) Here are the major ones:

- **Damn the Torpedoes**: This company wants to be different. If all the companies are doing X, they'll do Y. If everyone is using System

ABC, they'll choose system XYZ. The ethos can be summed up in this way: "I'm doing this because I want to, I'm doing it because it's a little naughty. I'm choosing to work with this company because nobody else is. I want to swim in the other direction. *Vive la différence!*"

• **David vs. Goliath:** When we first started, folks used to call my company, ICD, those "three guys in a van." The narrative is similar to how Hewlett-Packard was founded (in a one-car garage), or Apple (in Steve Jobs's parents' home and garage), or Facebook (in a dorm room). Some people dig that entrepreneurial spirit, and they want to be part of something new, something developing, something up and coming. The ethos is "I'm going with the little guy because I like to support the little guy. I don't like bullies. I don't want to be a cog in a big old wheel."

• **The Little Engine That Could:** If your company is the little guy, and you work hard and appreciate a client's business more than the big guys do, you might work the "little engine that could" angle. At ICD, we won a lot of business because we could say, "We're not JP Morgan or Goldman Sachs. You will be a significant client to us, and your business will truly matter. Your business will change our lives and provide real jobs to others. We're pure hustle, and we desperately need you to be happy." For the client, the appeal of this ethos is "I'm picking these hustlers because I want concierge service, and I like that our happiness is tied to their success. If we're not happy, we can fire these guys in one phone call."

• **Tried but True.** Those who don't want to stick their necks out, or embrace a rebellious or entrepreneurial spirit, or commit to the latest flavor or trend, will feel better going with a trusted product, a safe bet. Nobody ever got fired for buying a Xerox. If you're in a bigger company and can't make any of these "little guy" arguments, lean into the "tried and true" ethos: "We're reliable, we're trusted, we've been around for a thousand years. You know what you'll get, and we're not going to surprise you or go belly up."

At ICD, we relied on a combination of "David vs. Goliath" and "The Little Engine That Could" to woo our clients. Indeed, without the big financial institutions kicking sand in people's faces and treating their customers badly, we probably wouldn't have had a business. Our ethos was, in effect, "It begins with please and doesn't end with thank you. We'll treat you better, and your business moves the needle here. By doing business with us, you're actually providing jobs and helping our families."

5. Find Your Frame of Mind: That Buddha Guy Was Onto Something! The Buddha was a big fan of "mind over matter." As he once said:

> *We are what we think.*
> *All that we are arises with our thoughts.*
> *With our thoughts, we make the world.*

Frame of mind can determine where you end up—your attitude and your altitude. A positive frame of mind can be prophetic. A negative frame of mind can be equally prophetic. Here are some techniques, ideas, and principles to help improve yours:

Use Visualization. This is a strong mental preparedness tool, which informs and affects confidence and enthusiasm. Visualization is used in sports, business, and other areas where high performance is necessary. Picture a positive outcome—leading your client down the path to your product, for example—and there's a greater like-lihood of that actually happening. If you can foresee good things happening and believe that they'll happen, you have a better chance of making them happen.

Before a meeting or call, think to yourself, "Okay, here's what we're going to do," and take a minute to visualize the flow of the meeting: the agenda, how it begins, your key arguments and val-ue-added propositions, what problems you'll be solving, and how you close. As in chess or any game or sport, think a couple moves ahead. Imagine what your next play might be and use visualization to stay ready and fluid.

Once the meeting begins, don't use a script. Stay in tune with the agenda and key points that you want to drive home, but allow the meeting to evolve organically. The customer might shift the dialogue, so try not to get thrown off if your talk goes "3-2-1-4" instead of "1-2-3-4." Practice being able to improvise and still cover your main points. If you cultivate an overall belief in your capability to get back on track, you'll be able to make your main points in any order, like a master.

Channel the East. This discussion of "transfer of enthusiasm" has actually been going on for thousands of years. Several ancient con-cepts from Eastern cultures reflect similar ideas.

One is the Zen teachings of Huang Po on the "transmission of mind." Huang Po advocated avoiding "conceptual thinking" and returning to a "beginner's mind"—being eager to learn new things, which is helpful in finding a calm and open frame of mind.

You might also think of a transfer of enthusiasm as a trans-fer of energy. Consider the concept of one's "qi" (pronounced "chee")—a life essence or vital energy that animates the body internally. It consists of the opposite forces of "yin" and "yang," which make up all of existence, always transforming and adjusting to each other, but always in harmony. Yin and yang help us understand that one person's energy is connected to another's. As the balance or "transfer" of energy happens and your confidence grows, you might notice ripple effects beyond that transaction into the next deal, and the next.

As Sun Tzu once observed in his oft-quoted book *The Art of War*, "Opportunities multiply as they are seized."

6. Develop Pre-Meeting or Pre-Sales Call Tactics. How to put yourself into that right frame of mind? What routines will help you get ready to walk in the door? We covered similar techniques in **Chapter 3: F.A.C.E. the Day: Attitude**, but it bears repeating that adjusting your attitude can be essential when preparing for a sales call. These next strategies may seem simple, but they can make all the difference in a meeting being effective, average, or a bomb.

• **Listen to Upbeat Music.** My playlist is called "Fire Up" and includes songs such as AC/DC's "It's a Long Way to the Top (If You Wanna Rock 'n' Roll)" and Pete Townsend's "Let My Love Open the Door." Make your own playlist to fire yourself up.

• **Be Well-Dressed, Well-Rested, and in a Good Mood.** Act and dress the part, and it will boost your mood and transform yourself into someone people want to be around.

• **Use Positive Self-Talk.** Think of the things and people you love most and conjure those positive images before you go into a meeting. Use self-affirmations as self-talk, such as "I am ready" and "We are going to win."

7. Leverage Your "Value Added." Understanding how to extend the value of your products or services, and of yourself, can help your client become enthusiastic about an impending deal. This includes clarifying how your products or services can:

- Solve a problem for them
- Make them more effective at their job
- Save them time
- Save them money
- Make them money
- Make them look good in the eyes of their employer
- Keep them as a lifelong client

There's also the art of emphasizing the "opportunity cost" for *not* changing. How can they avoid the professional risks of not using your product? What is the potential danger in missing the boat? You can subtly push and pull all of these buttons and levers to make your client feel confident that they're making the right choice, keeping up with the Joneses, and not being the last kid on the block to take their training wheels off.

8. Harness Word of Mouth. Sometimes you can present your prospects with testimonials or case studies—other clients who have done business with you and can say nice things about you. Even better is when referrals and word-of-mouth buzz emerge organically to build enthusiasm. Sometimes this can happen if you arrange events in which different clients—past, present, and future—can get into conversation, making potential new clients feel confident in your products or services.

Another kind of enthusiasm comes from a growing reputation as you follow an individual person moving up in a company or hopping from one company to the next on the corporate ladder. For example, Bao Tran was my client at three different outfits before ultimately becoming the treasurer of the data-storage company Iron Mountain. He told me that when he arrived at each new place, one of the first calls he'd make was to ICD. It was an easy vendor decision because hiring us made him look good. Mr. Tran knew we were going to deliver, that gave him confidence, and everybody benefited.

At ICD we jokingly referred to our repeat customers as "repeat offenders," considering their loyalty the greatest form of flattery.

CHAPTER 12

ACTIVE LISTENING

EDibles: How I Learned to Shut Up and Harness the Power of Active Listening

"Hearing tells you that music is playing,
but listening tells you what the song is saying."
—ANONYMOUS

Listening is more critical now than ever before.

You might argue that since the rise of the digital world, the influence of salespeople has eroded. It's harder for an individual salesperson's presence to compete with the power of cell phones, texting, websites, email, the internet, and social media.

But there's one way in which the individual can still compete with all that "noise," and that's by being a good listener and taking action based on that listening. Until they invent better and scarier robots, listening is a skill that humans can do and your computer cannot. Just try talking to one of those AI-powered "voicebots" when you need a representative on the line: "Press '1' if you're angry. Press '2' if you're really angry."

Let's go back to the early days, 2003, when we had just launched ICD. We'd been selected by Home Depot to implement our money-market trading platform. The deal was going well, and we understood the company's pain points. We were sure they were going to go with us. Then, at the eleventh hour, we got snaked on the deal by a division of Bear Stearns, the monster global invest-ment bank. Bear Stearns swooped in with some significant players and tilted the scales, and we lost the bigger portion of the deal.

But that's not the end of the story. We still ended up winning the Canadian-currency portion of Home Depot's business because our competitor couldn't provide that service. It was about 5 per-cent of the business we could have had from the larger deal, but that piddling amount grew bigger the next year, because we kept engaging and listening to the client. Home Depot had an idea about a new feature they wanted for reporting their accruals and divi-dends. I took the idea to my partners, who approved it, and then to our technology team, who customized it for my client, stat. The solution we developed ended up exceeding what Home Depot was experiencing elsewhere with other vendors.

We continued to listen to their feedback, and we continued to evolve and develop our product, providing better reporting, refin-ing our front end, and improving the user interface. They liked it more and more and more. Ultimately, our product and service for one-twentieth of their business was far better than what our com-petitor provided for the whole company. Eventually, Home Depot moved the other 95 percent over to us.

The lesson of my Home Depot saga is that ICD ended up out-servicing the company who beat us, Bear Stearns, by carefully listening to our client. (Incidentally, Bear Stearns cratered during the 2008 global financial crisis and recession, and their remains were sold to JP Morgan Chase. May they rest in peace.)

Active Listening: The Core Principle

"Too often we underestimate the power of a touch, a smile, a kind word, a listening ear, an honest compliment, or the smallest act of caring, all of which have the potential to turn a life around."
—LEO BUSCAGLIA

What Is Active Listening and Why Is It Important? How you listen actively will vary by situation, but the key concept is this: active listening means being attentive and engaged in an affirmative way with the person (or people) in your conversation. Make the other party feel heard and valued. Don't interrupt, impose your own point of view, or pass judgment. Let the other person know you've paid attention. Keep your mouth shut.

Here are three principles to keep in mind:

• **Effective Listening *Is* Active Listening.** Despite this fact, active listening is not the norm, and it's not second nature for most of us. As Stephen Covey put it, "Most people don't listen with the intent to understand; they listen with the intent to reply." But you can't really understand what the other person is saying if you're occupied with finding a place to enter the conversation, waiting with bated breath to spill out your next brilliant thought. I'm guilty of this all the time.

• **Truly Listening to Somebody Is Not Easy.** This is not only a discipline, it represents a humble point of view. You're communicating that what the other party has to say is of value. Your role is to help them articulate what they want to say. Active listening is a kind of facilitating. Like a good talk-show host, the great listener not only facilitates the other side of the conversation but also inspires that person to speak with greater cogency, use better information, and provide smarter insights.

• **Active Listening Means You're Focused on Them, Not You.** Think about going to see a doctor: you'll always feel better when the doctor is really tuned into you. "How are you feeling? How can I help you? What can I do for you?"

The Six Benefits of Active Listening for Sales

"The word listen contains the same letters as the word silent."
—ALFRED BRENDEL

1. Active Listening Shows Good Business Etiquette. Like many of the other tools and techniques in this book, active listening is another way to flex your manners muscles and show respect to your business contacts. By listening well, you're engaging in polite and professional communication.

Like "please" and "thank you," active listening conveys—without any noise emanating from your lips— "I care about you. I hear you. I understand your point of view." In other words, active listening makes *you* look good. You're polite, you're attentive, you're patient. You adhere to the norms of a civilized world. Unlike all those barbarians out there, you're here to listen.

2. Active Listening Creates Positive Sales Energy. Yes, you are trying to make a sale. And a customer is there, perhaps, to buy something. But, as we've established, a fundamental truth about sales is that people don't want to be sold to. They want to buy something. Using active listening, you can change the dynamic from a sales presentation to a buying opportunity, and then you'll be more successful.

You're endeavoring to create an environment in which your prospect or client feels that they're heard. You want to present yourself as an open book, so that someone else can receive that energy, as opposed to making them suspicious or guarded because you're giving off a sleazy, salesperson vibe. Once they believe in your interest in them, they will want to buy (and buy again) from you. Active listening can create positive energy.

3. Active Listening Creates Trust. Listening to the words of another person is the only way to authentically generate trust; and if you can generate trust from your customer, then they're more likely to buy whatever is in front of them—whether it's ideas, a particular product, a service, or a way of doing things. You can gain a prospect's trust by making them feel heard.

4. Active Listening Creates Respect. The act of repeating back what somebody has said to you not only confirms your active listening, it's also a high form of respect. Most people love it when you repeat something they've told you in conversation. Echo one of their mantras or battle cries: "You've made it loud and clear that you 'need this thing to integrate with your treasury workstation,'" or "'I just want the damn thing to work.' We can do that." When you show respect, you demonstrate that you're worthy of being in a relationship with them.

5. Active Listening Makes You the Problem-Solver. Active listening is also related to a concept I discussed in **Chapter 8: Establishing Rapport** and **Chapter 9: Maintaining Relationships**: in any courtship of a prospect, you want to go way beyond simply trying to make a sale. You're solving a problem for that potential customer, and the only way you're going to do that is by listening carefully to all of their struggles and challenges.

Demonstrating empathy and understanding via active listening shows that a customer can rely on you as an expert, and that you will help them solve their problem. Then and only then can you become that person's trusted resource for ideas, which will lead to closing a deal and forming a powerful collaboration.

6. Active Listening Empowers Your Client (and You). Assigning power to a prospect or client is a convincing and concrete way to show that you understand how important they are. Active listening is another way of assigning power, as well as shifting the power dynamic from "Hey, listen to *me*" to "I want to listen to *you*." Ask *them* to describe the reason you're there. Have *them* tell you how you can help. Have *them* describe the problem you're there to solve. Most people love to be asked questions and to tell you their answers, with the spotlight turned on them. Ask questions. Then be quiet and listen.

While active listening is an empowering phenomenon for the person you're facing, it's also empowering for you, the salesperson. Why? Because it's the only way you can delve into the intimate details that this person wants to share with you, and establish a private and confidential relationship. After those personal exchanges, you'll have a greater opportunity to provide solutions or ideas because the person across the table has communicated something you wouldn't have known otherwise—the biggest frustration she has with her team, the biggest beef she has with her boss, the worst nightmare she's having with her current system. She won't tell you any of that if she doesn't trust you, and she won't trust you unless you're patient and listen attentively.

Listening has a compound effect. It creates reciprocity, helping them and helping you.

Active Listening: Putting the Principle into Play

"Listening is not merely hearing, it is receiving the message that is being sent to you. Listening is reacting. Listening is being affected by what you hear. Listening is letting it land before you react. Listening is letting your reaction make a difference. Listening is active."

—MICHAEL SHURTLEFF

Now that you understand why active listening is important, how do you actually do it effectively? As I said above, it's not a skill most of us do well. In a personal relationship, one partner might criticize the other for trying to solve their problems or for interrupting them as they talk rather than simply being silent and absorbing what they have to say.

The same applies to a business setting. It takes practice. We often have to consciously get into "listening mode." This means *not* offering judgment or your own point of view—that's where this skill differs from critical listening. Instead, let the other party be heard and give them an opportunity to fix their own issues (at least at first).

Here are eight ways to expand your capacity as an effective listener.

1. Clear Your Mind. Listen to yourself. You've got all of these voices in your head. According to Freud, in each person there are at least three major driving forces: the **id**, the primitive part of the mind whose goal is to meet your basic, instinctual needs ("Crap! Late for work. Must speed!"); the **ego**, which is a kind of reality check on the id, fluffing up your state of being and managing and protecting you ("Patient. Slow. Chill, dude."); and the **superego**, which adds a layer of critical thinking and morality ("Speeding is bad. I've already gotten seven speeding tickets this year."). All these versions of yourself are constantly bouncing around inside your skull. *Oh, I've got this idea. Oh no, hey, don't forget to do that. What will Mom think?*

That's a lot of noise. To be able to listen to somebody else, you have to clear the decks in your own head so that you're capable of listening; otherwise, you'll be stuck in "first person" and won't really be "there" in the meeting or conversation.

Listen to yourself, and do an audit of yourself. Being prepared to listen might require some mental and emotional calisthenics before you get into the conference room. Prepare to focus not on you but on the other party, so that you can understand what that other person is thinking and caring about. Listening is an internal thing. To do it, you need to tune out or quiet the noise in your own head.

2. Ask Questions That Facilitate Discussion. There are two main kinds of questions that will keep the conversation flowing.

Open-ended questions. These questions encourage and stimulate dialogue. Think of journalism's famous "Five Ws": "Who," "What," "When," "Where," and "Why" (and sometimes "How"). In a business setting, open-ended questions might be "Tell me what your budget is for this project," or "Why isn't your existing solution working for you now?" Each of these questions encourages thought and should require a longer answer than "Yes" or "No." Asking probing, open-ended questions will get your counterparts to talk about how to solve their problem.

If somebody is merely curious about a product that they're not ultimately going to buy, there's probably nothing you can do to change their mind. But if the person hasn't decided at the start of the conversation, asking them lots of questions will increase the likelihood that they'll buy something from you, because open-ended questions stimulate thought and conversation. They get the customer speaking about the virtues of the product and thinking about the problem you can solve.

Close-ended questions. These require one-word, "Yes" or "No" answers. Close-ended questions are generally used to gain clarity; to show the party that you understand their issue, problem, or struggle; or to get permission to move the sales process forward: "Can we reschedule this meeting for next Friday?" or "Are you prepared to choose our solution today?"

Asking clarifying, close-ended questions not only shows the client that you're listening to them but can also communicate a clear "tie-down" to a sale. If you're not an active listener, you might miss opportunities to ask these questions and tie down the sale.

3. Send Signals That You're Paying Attention. The most basic way to communicate "I'm listening" is by making eye contact. Studies show that eye contact projects confidence and self-esteem and makes you seem more likable and trustworthy. Of course, don't stare or be creepy and weird. But by looking directly and periodically into the eyes of the other person, or by using other cues like smiling and nodding, you'll feel connected and the other party will feel listened to. At least in Western cultures, not making eye contact implies that you're not to be trusted, that you have something to hide, or that you're not telling the truth.

Another way to confirm the fact that you're paying attention is to give short, verbal feedback at the right time. It might be a short statement to let the person know you understand the gravity of their situation: "I can see how that would be hard." Or use more subtle signals, like a nod or an "Uh-huh" or "Hmm" or "Yes, right."

These are also ways of getting small buy-ins: as you show enthusiasm about their issue, these verbal signals will subtly begin the transfer of enthusiasm (as we explored in **Chapter 11**).

4. Pick Up on Cues. We can learn a lot from what someone says, but don't neglect what isn't being said. Whether it's tone of voice, body language, eye contact, or a facial expression like a raised eyebrow or sleepy eyelids, non-verbal cues offer a wealth of information. You can usually sense another party's lack of attention, annoyance, boredom, confusion, or excitement, even in a Zoom conference.

Also, look for signs of how attentive the other person is feeling so that you can gauge how well *you're* doing at listening. If the signals look disheartening, ratchet up your listening technique. If your contact's mood began as sarcastic or angry but evolved to become more lighthearted or engaged, then you've made progress in listening well and perhaps breaking down their resistance.

Active listening also means picking up on things that are conspicuous by their absence. Why isn't this person talking much or mentioning a certain topic? Why are they leaving a certain person's perspective out? It might be because they don't understand something you've said, or maybe there's a deeper problem. Maybe there's pressure from a boss. Maybe it's another issue. You can ask questions to find out.

5. Take Notes. Two of the best tools for an active listener are a pen and paper. Taking notes shows that you're listening during the conversation and that you respect what the other party has to say, because you're writing it down. To a lesser extent, taking notes also shows the person that you're being honest; you're holding yourself and them to a record of what you're both saying.

Taking notes, moreover, shows that you're absorbing the person's comments, rather than just going through the motions or preparing your next point. It's a physical manifestation of being present in the room. Later, you can consult your notes to confirm what you've heard, showing the person, in a respectful way, that you've been engaged in the conversation the whole time. Ultimately, this tactic is another way to foster a sympathetic connection with the person you're meeting with.

6. Keep an Open Mind. Let's imagine that you're having a conversation with a potential client. You've done your due diligence, but you really don't know a person until you sit down with them. As you're actively listening, be creative and keep your mind open to potential directions for the conversation. A good salesperson is always calibrating.

If a conversation isn't going well, shift your goals from "Must make the sale" to something more modest: "Maybe I can get her to trust me," or "Maybe he can make a referral," or "Maybe I'm not going to close this guy, but if I get to know him a little better and he starts to trust me, maybe I can introduce him to somebody who will get him over the finish line later." Keeping an open mind means continually searching for where you're at with somebody. Listen to the words and picture what the speaker is saying; try to feel what they're expressing and understand what they're really thinking. Even if you can't make the sale, you can garner a clearer picture of a company or at least of that buyer. You're listening to the images they're creating, the problems they're elucidating, and if you can give them good feedback from that perspective, that's a step in the right direction.

7. Earn Permission to Speak and Collaborate. If you demonstrate that you're a genuine person who is engaged and listening, you'll be able to determine the proper time to talk and share your ideas.

As you're actively listening, look for clues—are they asking you what you think, or for suggestions based on your experience? You want permission to engage with the other person and to let them know where they need help, your take on a problem that they're having, and the way you might be able to solve it. You also want permission to solve it.

The speaker might grant you that permission explicitly, or it might happen organically, when the person feels safe enough to open up. You can't take permission unilaterally. Permission is a gift given to you. Listening can give you permission to respond to them, but it still has to be earned.

Return to basic manners. Wait for the speaker to pause. Ask questions to get the speaker's permission. "Would you like to hear my ideas? Is it okay if I share my thoughts with you?" You're giving them the power, so the communication becomes power-sharing too. As you sense the transfer of permission, you may sense that the person is stimulated by your enthusiasm. If they're excited about the possibility of working with you, you'll see that their own creative mechanism has been triggered. Ideas will start flowing both ways. Then you'll know that you've received permission for true collaboration.

This should go without saying, but you can't *will* anyone to be your client. No one will ever be your client, advocate, friend, or resource if you force yourself on them or try to manipulate them. Even if a prospect calls you, you still have to earn their permission to work with them. And if you don't listen carefully enough, you may miss not only the opportunity to speak but the entire reason you're there in the first place.

Remember, successful product development comes from using strong listening skills. It's crucial not just for shaping a product but for onboarding and winning new business. If you build something for Coca-Cola, there's a good chance Pepsi might need it too. Being able to listen can secure deals and lead to other opportunities.

8. Repeat, Restate, Reiterate. When you're done listening, mirror back what you've heard the other person say. Make sure you've got it right with a tie-down. "Here are the takeaways from our meeting. In our discussion today we discovered that these are your current deficiencies. Problem one, problem two, problem three. We're going to try to address those. Do we have that right?"

After the meeting, it can be helpful in some cases to send those present at the meeting a summary of your findings—again reinforcing your thoughtful, respectful, interested, active listening. Confirm in an email what they've said, as well as their timeline.

Active Listening: Don't Try This

"Before you act, listen. Before you react, think.
Before you spend, earn. Before you criticize, wait.
Before you pray, forgive. Before you quit, try."
—WILLIAM ARTHUR WARD

Don't Space Out. Here's a personal pet peeve: you're having a conversation with someone and they seem to be listening, but actually they're checking their phone, sneaking a look at the clock or someone else's screen, or, worst case, sending texts. If you want to be truly attentive, don't multi-task. Be fully present. Turn your damn phone off or leave it in the car.

Don't Interrupt. It's tempting when you're listening actively to immediately connect what's being said to your own experience.

"Wow. That reminds me of the time when I was a buyer for a clothing chain and had to manage our distribution center's inventory, issue purchase orders, and reconcile a million invoices. What a pain..." Pretty soon you're monologuing for fifteen minutes. Keep your part of the conversation to a minimum, and don't tell too many war stories.

Don't Offer Solutions (Too Soon). When I'm in a meeting, sometimes so many ideas are bubbling in my head that I need to work hard not to blurt them all out. While I love that feeling of an "explosion of ideas"—it means I'm really engaged—I still need to shut down that part of my mind.

Similarly, sometimes we get so excited that we start planning the victory parade before we've even won the game. Don't jump the gun. I tell myself, "I need to close my mouth. I need to become quiet and still so that I can hear the other person." If I must speak, I wait for a pause in the conversation. If I have any brainstorms, I jot them down in my notes and use those gems later in the conversation.

4

MODES OF
COMMUNICATION

CHAPTER 13

PHONE

EDibles: Smashingly Well, or Surprisingly Badly

> "Anybody have plans to stare at their phone
> somewhere exciting this weekend?"
> —NITYA PRAKASH

Over my lifetime, I have made and answered hundreds of thousands of phone calls. These interactions can go smashingly well, or surprisingly badly. Your relationship can get off on the right foot, or that foot can be firmly planted in someone's mouth.

If you've ever been solicited via phone, you can relate. You know how hard it can be for the salesperson to come off as genuine and not forced or desperate. Sometimes, even if the salesperson has a great product to sell, their phone manner can be off-putting or seem fake.

But, done well, a phone call can launch, strengthen, or even save a business relationship.

In March of 2008, during the financial crisis, I had a client named Bob Williams, a treasury professional who at the time worked for the Interpublic Group of Companies (IPG). Bob had to answer IPG's senior management's most pressing question, "Are we comfortable with our sizable short-term money-market trades clearing through Bear Stearns?" Bear Stearns was having difficulties, and people didn't know if they were going to be around much longer.

As Bob tells the story, I stepped in, using phone-based communications to help him through the crisis. The weekend before JP Morgan took over that part of the business for Bear Stearns, Bob and I were talking constantly on the phone, Friday night through Sunday. I sent Bob a presentation deck explaining the risks that all our clients were facing and how ICD had it covered. We believed there was minimal settlement risk with Bear Stearns, but I continued to monitor the situation as the weekend went on.

Bob knew his entire career was hanging in the balance. Being in touch with me, even though he was in New York City and I was in Boston, meant that he could communicate frequently with his senior management in a way that gave them comfort and confidence and allowed them to stay the course.

"What am I going to do?" he said to me. "We're just the little guy."

"Listen," I assured him, "all of our clients have a seat at the table."

ICD got him through the crisis, and IPG made it through, thanks to good old-fashioned telephone communication and etiquette.

And just think: we never texted each other once. Sometimes there's no substitute for real-time, one-on-one phone contact.

Phone Versus Email: The Core Principle

"Wise men speak because they have something to say,
fools because they have to say something."
—PLATO

Before we discuss telephone etiquette in particular, let's focus on how a phone call and an email differ. As we'll also see in **Chapter 14: Email**, each method of communication has its own etiquette and effectiveness, and there are rationales for why you'd use one instead of the other in different situations.

Like other skills discussed in this book, using email and calling people on the phone are ways to express polite and professional courtesy. You can use these communication tools to project an image of yourself as attentive, efficient, dependable, knowledgeable, helpful, detail-oriented, and eager to get down to work. Consider your goals during the initial contact phase and what your desired impact should be. Your email and phone style is another way to communicate who you are. How you conduct yourself, not only in person but also in these other realms, contributes to the success of your business connections and influences how well you, your product, your team, and your company are received.

Email or Phone Call? Here are my thoughts on the use of email versus the use of the phone in business dealings.

Phone communication used to be more formal, but it's become casual in recent years. In the world of business, access to an individual is now easier and more direct. It's common to have a person's direct line or mobile number, and less necessary to placate executive assistants who are screening calls. The downside? Your call is more likely to go straight to voicemail.

Remember the formal business letter, that 8½-by-11-inch piece of paper folded in thirds and sent in the mail? Email, a comparatively casual mode of communication, has taken its place. Yes, email makes communication quicker and easier, but it's also become a huge time suck because we have access to it 24/7. Today the average employee spends approximately one quarter of their workday going through their email. I used to call people to set up meetings. Nowadays business people set up meetings, discuss issues, and confirm decisions via email.

Perhaps there's a cultural or generational shift happening: those who are digital natives, who grew up texting and emailing, may not feel as comfortable speaking to a live human on the phone. In some ways, I get it. Emailing is easier. You can hide behind an email. But you definitely will have more impact and success as a salesperson if you use the telephone instead of emailing.

That said, I think it's important to be able to do both. Mix it up. If you've been conducting a relationship mostly by email for weeks or months, it won't hurt to call the person and express niceties at the beginning of the conversation to build rapport. I'll often say something like my signature greeting: "Hola! Where do we find you on the planet today?" I'll check in, ask a question, or share some of my own personal news. Then I'll get to the purpose of my call. Email, of course, has benefits of its own; for one thing, when you use email the record of your interaction—who agreed to what—is automatically archived "in writing."

We'll talk about texting and video conferencing later. For now, when choosing between using email or phone, especially when prospecting or making cold calls, here are some factors to consider:

• **The Client's Preference.** What method of communication does your prospect or client prefer? You may not know the answer at first, but heed any preference they express.

• **Your Time and Budget.** Calls are more personal and warmer than emails, but making calls takes time and, on the receiving end, can come off as invasive. On the other hand, you can easily send hundreds of emails cheaply and efficiently, but they're easily deleted or avoided.

• **Your Style and Personality.** Phone calls create a real, live, human interaction and help you build rapport. You can improvise and adapt your conversation or sales pitch as needed. Customers find it harder to refuse your offer if you're live on the phone. Email, by contrast, is more of a one-sided communication, but if you're not as good at talking on the fly, using email allows you to prepare your words ahead of time.

• **The Purpose of Your Communication.** Phone calls are better for complicated explanations or apologies, when you want to make a big "ask" or need to close a deal, or need an immediate reply. Email is ideal for simple tasks, like following up or conveying something that needs to be "in writing." It's also better for when you need to send messages to multiple members of a team at once, or to send visual images, lots of data, or financial information or documents.

Think of phone and email as two different building blocks that will help you construct your first impression, establish rapport, form a lasting relationship with a client or prospect, and ultimately facilitate your sales performance. Just remember: when using either medium, you need to be mindful and polite and use your phone and email powers for good, not evil.

Phone: Putting the Principle into Play

From how to use your best phone manner to leaving a clever voicemail, here are a few tips for executing killer phone calls in support of your sales career.

Making Calls

"People used what they called a telephone because they hated being close together and they were scared of being alone."
—**CHUCK PALAHNIUK**

There's an art to your phone manner. Practice makes perfect (and if you're making a ton of cold calls, you'll get plenty of practice). If you're rusty, it's okay to crib from a script.

• **Do Identify Yourself.** "Hi, this is Sarah Connor, sales manager from Cyberdyne Systems. Is this Kyle Reese?" If the respondent does not give their own name, or if it's unclear who has picked up the phone, say, "I'm sorry. Who am I speaking with?"

• **Do Greet the Other Party.** Thank the person who answered the phone. Always address the person on the other end as Mr. or Ms., until given permission to do otherwise. As I've said, I find it rude when people use my first name without my permission. I consider it a strike against the caller.

• **Do Find Quiet Time.** Call from a quiet location with limited background noise and interruptions. Avoid car or airport noises, barking dogs, crying kids, barking kids, or anything that might make you seem amateurish. Don't eat or drink during the call or make clicking sounds on your keyboard. Mute your audio when these distractions are unavoidable.

• **Do Be Clear.** Speak clearly and directly into the phone receiver. If you're using an over-the-ear headset, in-ear headset, earphones, or earbuds, test them before going live. (And remember, if you're using earbuds outside and speaking out loud, you're more likely to look like a person one brick short of a full load who's talking to yourself.)

• **Do Use Humor.** If someone unexpectedly picks up the phone and you're surprised to get a human, use a joke to pivot. Say something like, "I was not prepared to speak to an actual live human," or "What a shame. I had drafted a beautiful voicemail. Now I'm actually going to have to speak like a real person."

• **Do Engage Your Listener.** Just as with public speaking, start with an opener or something to engage the other person, so that they'll listen to the rest of what you have to say. Find the right balance between being formal and respectful and being clever and funny. Use the techniques discussed in **Chapter 12: Active Listening** to send signals that you're engaged with the other party's side of the conversation, and respond to their concerns. It's important to have your goals for the call in front of you, to stay on task.

• **Do Use Your Speakerphone Discreetly.** Ask permission of the caller before switching to speakerphone. Don't ever put the call on mute and then comment on the caller; this could get you into terrible trouble. Assume they can always hear you. The same goes for after a caller "drops off" a conference call. Assume that everyone is still on until you have hung up the phone.

• **Do End the Call.** It's important not to forget to disconnect at the end of the call. It would be a fatal mistake to speak about the person as if they were off the call when they are still listening.

Leaving Messages

"The telephone gives us the happiness of
being together yet safely apart."
—MASON COOLEY

If you want someone to return your call, leave a clear and con-
cise phone message. As I discussed in **Chapter 3: FACE the Day:
Attitude**, smiling when you speak helps to create an upbeat tone.
A message creates a record, shows persistence, and gets the ball
rolling. Just don't leave a message every day for a week. Some tips:

• **Do Leave a Message.** If the person is unavailable, leave a brief,
respectful voicemail (again, include your first and last name, job
title and/or company, and phone number). Speak clearly and slowly,
and pause between each part of your message.

• **Do Say When to Call Back.** Propose a time period, such as morn-
ings, Tuesdays through Thursdays, or whenever is best for reaching
you. Mention your time zone.

• **Do Use Humor.** This can be especially helpful if you're leaving multiple voicemails over a period of time. Humor can lighten the mood,
poke fun at the fact that the recipient might be avoiding you, lower
the pain threshold of receiving one of your messages, and leave them
chuckling. Maybe they'll be amused, take pity on you, and think,
"Aw heck, this person's been leaving me messages every week for a
month, and they keep getting funnier and funnier. Maybe I'll call her
back just to get this person off my list." Some examples:
  ◦ "This is the ever-persistent Bob Smith calling again."

- "In case you were wondering, I've been released from the witness protection program."
- "In the event that *you* have been taken into the witness relocation program, you can respond by barking like a dog, and I'll understand."
- "Just following up, as I know you spent the weekend curled up next to the fire reading our materials. I hope they did not end up in the fire. I'm sure our prospectus helped you sleep. A real page-turner!"
- "Our brochure is the crystal meth, Ritalin, or Adderall of marketing collateral."

• **Be Thankful.** Think of your message as a way to express your thanks and appreciation. Let the person know you appreciate their time and the effort it will take to call back. "Thanks for calling back at your earliest convenience," or "I know you're busy, so I appreciate your kindness in returning my call when you can. Thank you, Phil."

Receiving Calls

"The telephone, which interrupts the most serious conversations and cuts short the most weighty observations, has a romance of its own."
—**VIRGINIA WOOLF**

When the phone rings, you want to sound appreciative of the caller and make sure they have your full attention (hint: close your Facebook newsfeed). Here are some suggestions for sounding professional and eager as you pick up the phone.

• **Do Pick Up Quickly.** Answer by the second ring if possible, and no later than the third. Wait for an answer before placing a caller on hold, and ask their permission before doing so. If now is not a good time to take the call, immediately propose a time when you will return their call: "Could I give you a call on Thursday?"

• **Do Identify Yourself.** Answer the phone by identifying yourself with your first and last name, and your job title and/or company.

• **Do Answer the Phone with Confidence.** Speak clearly, with a positive, energetic tone, and loudly enough for your caller to hear you. Using the "smiling" technique can help to convey a positive attitude.

• **Do Be Grateful.** Even if you're in the middle of something, juggling a million things, having a lousy day, and watching your goldfish Nemo McPhelps float belly up in his bowl, do your best to fake it. Make the caller feel respected, important, and valued. Don't sound like it's an inconvenience to have them on the line with you. When you've got a live caller on the line, make it count.

• **Do Listen.** When receiving calls from prospects and clients, listen attentively to their questions and concerns, acknowledge them, and apologize if appropriate. Be authentic. When clients call, they may require immediate answers or action, and they might be a little pissed off. Get their name, their number, and the message. Assure them that you will get to the bottom of the situation and that they'll get a call back by a specific time. For example, "I will personally call you back," or "The appropriate team-member will call you back by noon today."

Other Tips on Phone Etiquette

"So that's the telephone? They ring, and you run."
—EDGAR DEGAS

Whether you use a landline or a mobile, here are the basics of good phone manners:

• **Do Return Any Calls as Soon as Possible.** It doesn't look good for the company or for your team if you don't return calls. One of my mentors, the great Mark Casady, had a policy of returning any phone call or email within twenty-four hours, no matter what. Mark was a massively successful CEO multiple times over. I tend to follow his philosophy.

• **Do Follow Through on Any Phone Requests**. Make good on any requests or messages. Forward a document, set up a meeting in a timely fashion, and so forth.

• **Do End the Call on a Positive Note.** Thank the person for calling and say good-bye, but let the caller hang up first.

• **Do Take Any Message Correctly.** Get the name, the number, the day and time of the call, and the details of the message—and be accurate.

• **Do Apologize If You Screw Up.** Sometimes you'll disconnect a caller when putting them on hold or transferring a call internally. If possible, take the person's name and phone number prior to transferring them, so that, if the call gets disconnected, you can call them back immediately.

• **Do Have an Appropriate Voicemail Greeting.** Use your own voice, identifying your name and company and when you are generally reachable. Never use the default "You have reached 123-555-1212" greeting on your business line. Callers may be reluctant to leave a message if your outgoing message is not personalized, because they may feel unsure if they've reached the correct person or an actual human being.

About Mobile Phones

"Cell phones are so convenient that they're an inconvenience."
—HARUKI MURAKAMI

Of course, some offices still use landlines, but increasingly employees are doing business on mobile phones (either their own or ones provided by their employers). And while mobiles still work as phones, because of all the cool bells and whistles built into them they require special care and feeding, so that you don't become distracted from your primary goal, which should be professional and polite business communication. Here's some specialized advice about their uses and potential misuses:

• **Do Stow Your Device.** Don't leave your mobile on the table during a meeting. Turn it off before your meeting begins, put it in airplane mode (or, at the least, vibrate mode), or leave it at your desk.

• **Don't Use Your Phone in Meetings.** Never use your phone during a meeting unless its use is pertinent to the meeting. That means no texting, no social media, and no internet during any in-person business gatherings (and that includes the "hiding it under the table" trick). The glowing screen is disruptive, and your distracted attention will be perceived as rude.

• **Do Leave the Room for Phone Calls.** If you're expecting a call that you must take, inform the attendees upon joining the meeting. Then, when your phone rings, leave the room rather than interrupt the meeting.

• **Do Be Discreet.** There are few things more annoying and less professional than someone carrying on a business conversation on the treadmill at the gym or at a bar in an airport. Be aware of your surroundings and keep your conversations to yourself.

• **Don't Raise Your Voice.** It may seem that you need to speak more loudly when on your mobile, but you don't. Those microphones are sensitive. No need to yell.

About Text Messages

"Our mobile devices are so powerful that they don't just change what we do, they're changing who we are."
—SHERRY TURKLE

In terms of business communications, to me a text is a cross between a phone call and an email. It can be as informal and intimate as an actual verbal chat or call with someone, but it's also a form of written communication, like email, with the ability to attach photos and send links. People are much more likely to look at a text than an email. Why? Because right now people have their eyeballs on their phones. They may not want to talk to people, but they're messaging each other back and forth, sending both personal and business-related texts, 24/7.

Formal communication around a business transaction usually needs to be carried out via a phone call or an email. But this expectation is changing. One study showed that prospects who received text messages converted at more than twice the rate of the average contacted lead (note: this only worked after first being contacted on the phone). So, depending on your relationship with your business associate and their preference, appropriate texting may be acceptable and can even be leveraged for developing business relationships.

Certainly, once you've established rapport with a client, texting is a quick, ideal medium for arranging a golf meeting or a dinner. Say you're at the restaurant and you want to say, "Our table's in the corner." But remember, follow the lead of your client in asking for or offering a work or personal cell number.

Overall, it seems clear that barriers are slowly coming down around informal cell-phone use and texting in the business world.

Pandemic Protocols:
Video Conferencing in the Age of the Coronavirus

"What are the benefits of speaking to your fans via email? It's quicker, easier, and involves less licking." —**Douglas Adams**

Since meeting in person has become difficult or impossible due to social-distancing guidelines and remote working practices, companies and sales forces are increasingly using video conferencing—often from a home office—as a way to stay in touch with prospects, clients, and teams. (You've probably noticed that most of your business associates are using their personal mobile phones more often than their office landlines.) As a result, the boundary between home and office is blurring even further.

As a salesperson, you'll soon realize that video conferencing adds another twist to your meeting prep routine. You need to be ready, well-dressed, and (if you're working from home) "broadcasting" from a location a few steps up from "the nook between the furnace and the hot-water heater."

That said, video has its advantages over phone and email as a way to stay in touch. I mean, sometimes you just need to see the smiling face of Brenda in corporate (based in Des Moines) or sales manager Todd (who lives only fifty miles away but is more fun to razz when you can see his face). Hence the proliferation of tele-conferencing tools and apps, and the ensuing nationwide panic as everyone scrambles to be as "good" on video as on phone, email, text, and telepathy. We're also learning how to be tolerant of visual and auditory distractions—like kids wandering amok in and out of the frame. Remember, we're all in this together.

Here are some tips on video-conferencing etiquette, to bring you up to speed:

• **Do Be Prepared.** You can have your notes on the screen, and no one else needs to see them. But be ready to "screen share" documents, PDFs, spreadsheets, or PowerPoint slides as needed. Make sure you know how to work the features of the video-conference software (especially if you're running the meeting and it's your first time).

• **Do Present Yourself Professionally.** Sit up straight, preferably at a desk rather than lounging on your bed surrounded by your Yorkshire terriers and their favorite pillows. Dress appropriately for work, not play. Frame your camera so that your head and torso are centered in the screen, at eye level to the lens.

• **Do Set Up Your TV "Studio" Space.** Choose a plain white wall or a neutral space, like an empty conference room or your home office. Use a headset for better sound quality. Have adequate lighting, and make sure your screen image doesn't have any creepy shadows or a grainy resolution. You may need to invest in a lighting solution specially designed for remote working. Don't use goofy green screens and virtual backdrops.

• **Do Mute Yourself When You're Not Speaking.** This is key in preventing any background racket or white noise from leaking into the call.

• **Do Interrupt Gracefully.** Some video-conferencing apps have a "raise your hand" feature or a chat channel for when you want to say something. If they don't, you may need to "barge in" from time to time—so do it tactfully.

• **Do Attempt to Make "Eye Contact."** Don't look at the image of the person you're speaking to. To provide the illusion of eye contact, look directly into your web camera (often located at the top of your computer monitor).

• **Do Be Respectful.** Pay attention to the other participants. Don't check your email or type during a meeting—it's pretty obvious when you're doing that (unless you're "away" and have blocked your video).

CHAPTER 14

EMAIL

EDibles: Don't Put the Cart
Several Miles in Front of the Horse

"Remember, anything you send electronically lives on forever."
—MARK HEYNER, CHIEF TECHNOLOGY OFFICER, ICD

Emails can be both an opportunity and a danger zone. How many of us have sent an email too early, before it was complete, cc'd the wrong person (this is one of my special gifts), or drafted a lengthy diatribe and then forgotten to send that bad boy altogether? I've made all those moves, and sometimes I layer mistakes on top of each other.

In this chapter, I'll identify some of the major pitfalls that I've fallen into and also describe some winning strategies for email. As with all of this book, pick whatever catches your eye and develop your own style.

We've all been on the receiving end of emails that seem "off." Imagine that you receive an email from a business contact saying, "Hey bro! How's it hanging?" or "Hey girlfriend!" The tone is far too chummy or chatty, considering that you haven't even met the contact in person or spoken on the phone yet. They've put the cart several miles in front of the horse. Your Spidey senses are triggered. You suspect that something about the person is unprofessional or untrustworthy, which might mean that their product or entire company is unreliable, even if you can't quite put your finger on it.

But when someone emails in a polite and appropriate way, you tend to read what they have to say, comply, and respond favorably, being courteous in return. And when you're the one who's writing the email and behaving courteously, the person on the other side will also respond in kind.

Like in-person dialogues and phone or video calls, email (and texting) is a two-way street, creating an open line of polite, professional communication that will help you build rapport and expand the networks of associations that lead to sales.

(Note: for "The Core Principle" of email, see "Phone Versus Email: The Core Principle" in **Chapter 13: Phone**.)

Email: Putting the Principle into Play

"A bad email reputation is like a hangover: hard to get rid of, and it makes everything else hurt
—**CHRISTOPHER MARRIOTT**

Email is another powerful tool for boosting your business relationships and sales success. To craft professional emails while avoiding some of the pitfalls I describe below—*spoiler alert: no emojis, please!*—here's my top advice:

• **Create the Right Tone.** An email is very similar to a letter—you write a greeting, compose a message, and sign it with your name. Your use (or misuse) of email will affect how you're perceived. The first email you send to someone—prospect, client, customer, employer—will help to form the recipient's first impression of you. If you offend someone in the salutation or body of the email, that person may not read any further. It may also influence that person's opinion of you. First impressions from emails are just as important as first impressions in person. Don't start off on the wrong foot.

• **Be Exceedingly Polite.** Try to write an email through the lens of the reader. It's never a problem to be over-polite. It's a big problem, however, when you're under-polite, presumptive, or rude. Understand that the recipient's mood, their work load, and their perception of your request all factor into how your email will be interpreted. Ask yourself, "How would I receive this email?" before you send it.

• **Stay on Top of Your Inbox.** Set aside time to look at your email each day. If you don't read messages in a timely fashion, you'll get left in the dust. If you can't reply right away, at least acknowledge the receipt of an email as soon as possible; for example, "Thanks, got your message. I will circle back soon."

> "Whatever you can say in a meeting you can put in an email.
> If I have questions, I'll tell you via email."
> **—MARK CUBAN**

SUBJECT LINES AND SALUTATIONS. Knowing the best greeting to use when crafting an email will enable you to create a positive first impression. When used properly, subject lines and salutations help you stand out in overflowing inboxes.

• **Do Use a Subject Line.** Make it clear and direct so the recipient can scan their emails and see "Quick favor," "Coming to town," "Killer event," "Networking opportunity," "Feedback requested," Time sensitive," or "DO NOT OPEN."

• **Do Use Proper Salutations**. Keep them simple but professional. Determine if the email should take an informal or formal tone, based on your prior correspondence and relationship with the person. Use "Mr." or "Ms." in a formal greeting (assuming you've confirmed the gender of the person). Other options are "Good afternoon," "Hello," or, if the recipients are of the same gender, "Good morning, ladies," or "gentlemen," or "gents." The old stand-by "Dear" looks strange in an email and is really not appropriate anymore.

• **Do Err on the Side of Formal**. Don't use informal greetings like "Hey Chuck," unless you know the person's comfort level with you using their nickname.

EMAIL BODIES. It's crazy how many emails I get in one day. Employees often get bogged down in checking their emails, which often becomes an unproductive use of time. Communicate efficiently and be respectful of the recipient's time.

• **Do Be Brief and Clear.** Keep your emails as brief and to the point as possible. Don't be too wordy, or no one will read it. Acknowledge any previous conversations or messages: "Thanks, I got your message"; "Just circling back to our conversation from last week"; "Here's the quote you requested." You can always attach a document or link to webpages with additional information.

• **Do Make the Text Easy to Read.** Use bullet points, highlight important words in bold, and use tags like "action item" to make sure that your recipient sees key information.

• **Do Write Professionally.** Some people assume because email is a less formal form of communication, you don't need to pay attention to the rules of proper English. Use complete sentences, appropriate grammar, and standard spelling and punctuation. Also, maintain a proper tone in your email; you don't want to come across as authoritative, impatient, or rude. For example, writing "You don't have to respond to this email right now" can come across as bossy.

CLOSINGS AND SIGNATURES. It's polite to add a simple closing at the end, to signal that your message has ended. A signature line below that ensures that your contact info and affiliations are crystal clear.

• **Do Close the Email.** For example, "Thanks for taking a look," or "I appreciate your time," followed by "Best regards," "All the best," "Kind regards," etc. Avoid such closings as "Sent from my iPhone," abbreviations like "TU" (thank you), or old-fashioned closings like "Sincerely yours" or "Faithfully yours."

• **Do Use a Signature Line.** It's important to embed your business signature in your email, including your name, your title, the name of your company, your direct number, your email address, the company website, your social media links, and potentially your company logo and/or awards and accolades. I typically reveal my personal cell number and social media info only internally or to trusted clients.

BEFORE SENDING. It's remarkably common for someone to inadvertently send an email before it's properly edited. A good salesperson may be selling a tremendous product, but if their email is riddled with errors or sent to the wrong person, they'll appear unprofessional.

• **Do Confirm Addresses and Details.** Sending an email to someone with the same first name or first letters of an email address can be very embarrassing. At my "advanced age," with my eyesight failing, this is becoming a more common mistake for me. Triple-confirm that the recipients' email addresses are correct.

• **Don't Type In the Person's Email Address Until the Email Is Ready.** I have been both the victim and the perpetrator of an email that wasn't completed. One way to avoid mistakes is to put your own name in the "To:" line, or nothing at all, until your email is properly vetted and ready to be sent.

• **Do Proofread.** Re-read your emails carefully with an eye for errors, and/or use your email software's spelling/grammar check before sending. Confirm that the subject line is correct, brief, and pertinent.

• **Do Avoid Emojis and Informal Abbreviations.** In writing professional emails, another potential pitfall is using emojis, emoticons (like ;-) to convey a wink and a smile), or informal acronyms (LOL, IMHO). Also, don't send memes like a picture of Leonardo DiCaprio from *The Wolf of Wall Street* captioned with "Was all this legal? Absolutely not!" Let's save those fun little gems for texts.

• **Do a Final Formatting Check.** Keep your fonts standard—nothing weird or hard to read, like a magenta-colored gothic or pirate font or, god forbid, Comic Sans. Don't type in all caps. For any reason. Ever. It's just bad form, and makes you look like a screaming idiot. DO YOU KNOW WHAT I MEAN????!!!!!

• **Do Check Your Attachments.** Be sure to include the correct attachment as well as confirm that it's actually needed; if it is, attach the correct, latest version of the document. Before sending it, open the document to be sure that you've attached the right one.

Other Tips on Email Etiquette

"Don't drive angry."

—PHIL, BILL MURRAY'S CHARACTER FROM *GROUNDHOG DAY*

• **Do Be Patient.** Don't be a pest if you don't get an immediate response to your email. Give it two or three days. Then you can follow up (unless you've received an out-of-office message).

• **Do Be Kind.** Don't send confrontational emails or respond to insulting messages. Sending an email in an angry state rarely works out. Breathe, wait, walk around the block—do anything but press "Send" when you're truly pissed off. Never write anything negative about anyone in an email. Inflammatory emails can and will come back to haunt you. Once you put something in writing in a company email, it is no longer confidential. I always try to operate as if anything I send will be read by the worst possible person. Also, don't use email as a way to avoid in-person or difficult discussions.

• **Do Be Aware of Cultural Differences.** Consider your audience. When emailing people from other countries or cultures, be cognizant that they may speak or write differently. For example, whereas in the US dates are—inexplicably—written "month/day/year" (9/29/1966), pretty much everywhere else on the planet dates are—logically—written "day/month/year" (29/9/1966).

• **Do Send Your Email Judiciously**. Proceed with caution when using "Reply All," and do so only if your message pertains to everyone on the thread or relates to a meeting, conversation, or business dealing that's relevant to all the people involved. Don't hit "Reply All" if you want the email to go only to the sender.

CHAPTER 15

SOCIAL MEDIA

EDibles: Adapt to the Tools of the Times

"A lot of people say that social media
is making us all dumber, but I not think that."
—ANONYMOUS

At the start of my career, social media didn't exist. At all. Neither did the internet, selfies, instant messaging, smart phones, Google, podcasts, YouTubers, Wikipedia, or SEO specialists. Or, for that matter, Swiffer, CrossFit, safe playground equipment, or gender-reveal parties.

I came into the financial services business as social media began. Before we got to Facebook, Instagram, LinkedIn, Twitter, and WeChat, we endured MySpace, Friendster, and LiveJournal. Anyone remember AOL or Sixdegrees.com? Usenet? The telegraph? Stone and chisel?

The point is not to call attention to my age—ahem, I mean my *experience*—but rather to say that, as a business person, you need to adapt to the tools of the times. Each generation has its own methods of communication, and in the case of business dealings each generation invents a new twist on how to connect with customers and clients. Back in the age of *Mad Men*, businesspeople used Rolodexes and three-martini lunches to prospect and schmooze. In 2020, the in-person confab, phone call, and handwritten note still get the job done, but we also have email, texting, and video conferencing at our disposal.

And then there's the very powerful and occasionally frivolous tool of social media to add to your tool-kit.

As Hamlet would say, "Ay, there's the rub." How can a salesperson use social media with a positive effect? Can one's use of it remain in keeping with good manners, smart etiquette, and polite and professional communications? Whether we're talking about corporate and company use or your own personal use of social media, what is the equivalent of "please" and "thank you" in the realm of posts, tweets, and likes?

> "Social media is not just a spoke on the wheel of marketing.
> It's becoming the way entire bicycles are built."
> **—RYAN LILLY**

Not to sound like the old guy in the room, but social media has contributed to the corruption of our manners and degraded basic communication between people. Our social media environment has disassembled the rules of the road. It's now much easier to take down an inappropriate uncle or bicker with an old colleague, staying safe behind an impersonal, high-speed internet connection, without ever having to face that uncle or colleague in person. Personally, I'm often bothered by people clamoring for attention on social media: "Come look at me! Admire my fabulous life! Here is my meal in Sardinia with my gorgeous, Ivy-League-bound offspring!"

That said, I'm as guilty as the next person. I feel conflicted about my own participation in social media and more than a little resentful of how easily it captures my attention. Too often I'm sucked into the rabbit hole of stupidity, foolishness, and mindless content—be it vapid celebrity nonsense, sports gossip, or the endless flow of market information. The mad wizards behind the curtain have clearly mastered how to dole out the perfect dose of psychological dopamine—something new or interesting, someone's response to you, someone's positive feedback in the form of a like or love—to keep us coming back for more. In the prescient words of T.S. Eliot, who never knew the internet, we are "distracted from distraction by distraction."

I heard a great line the other day with regard to social media: "If you're not being sold a product online, you are the product being sold." Meaning: your information, patterns, and movements within social media are being sold to someone on the other side.

But social media is evolving in front of us, and I think it's important to have a presence there. As I've said earlier, the mission of this book is to encourage the use of timeless and valuable techniques that convey respect, gratitude, and appreciation in your business communications and sales processes—ideas that have (for now) been swept under the rug. And even social media can be our friend in this effort.

Social Media: The Core Principle

"A brand is no longer what we tell the consumer it is—
it is what consumers tell each other it is."
—SCOTT COOK

There are many social media platforms to choose from, and the options can seem overwhelming. Many of us know the big three—Facebook, Twitter, and LinkedIn. You may also have personal experience with Instagram, Pinterest, and YouTube, as well as WhatsApp, Snapchat, Reddit, Medium, TikTok, and WeChat, not to mention starting your own blog or podcast.

One piece of advice that I was given early, when I started my own firm, EPBComms, was this: "The wise man knows what he knows not." Don't try to master everything or be all things to all people. Don't waste time trying to be an expert in twenty-seven different platforms. Pick the ones most relevant to your business, where your customers, audience, or constituents hang out, and focus on those. If you're not sure, seek the advice of a hired gun, like a digital-content manager or consultant, to help you decide where and how to establish your social media presence.

Personally, I don't have a Facebook profile, though my company does. Facebook, Twitter, and LinkedIn (which I do use) are the most important platforms for businesspeople like me, especially LinkedIn, which is built for content related to the workplace, jobs, and careers and is designed for networking. (I can also tell you that Facebook, Twitter, and LinkedIn have been clients of my firm.)

Three Reasons to Post on Social Media

"It's not just about consuming content,
but sharing it, passing it on, and adding to it."
—ARIANNA HUFFINGTON

Here are my three general principles for the smart care and feeding of social media for business people:

• **Post with a Reason**. Social media can be seductive, and your social media persona can become an exaggerated version of who you are. In a recent survey, 57 percent of Americans said they've posted something on social media that they later regretted. Watch your content. Be mindful of the pointless, goofy, or inappropriate.

Watch the vanity, the bragging, the gratuitous display of opinions. As a wise person once said, "What happens on social media stays on Google forever." Facebook and Instagram have no warning labels, but perhaps they should—or at least they should be hooked up to a Breathalyzer.

• **Post within Reason.** Don't upload photos or videos pointlessly or constantly. Think about quality versus quantity. Consider what you're communicating, how you're communicating, how often you're communicating, and through what channels you're communicating. Think about the purpose of your digital presence, and why you're posting what you're posting, before the entire planet can see it, hear it, read it, watch it, or be offended by it.

• **Post with Pride.** If you're a salesperson, when you're on social media you are in the public domain. You are also the face of your company for the people you're communicating with. If you say something out of bounds or controversial—like criticizing your company or a colleague, posting offensive content, or attacking others—it's going to be found out and you're going to get called onto the carpet by your constituents or your boss. If you're a salesperson for Pepsi, don't recommend "Rum and Cokes" on Instagram.

Keep in mind, there are now only a handful of companies who own and manage internet data—Facebook owns Instagram, Google owns YouTube, LinkedIn is owned by Microsoft. Not to go all Orwellian here, but there's reason for concern that the control of our information lies in very few hands. Be mindful that these big companies are gathering data about you and your every move on the internet, and that they have the power to censor or shut down your account if you abuse their policies. Buyer, beware!

Social Media: Try This

"On Twitter, we get excited if someone follows us.
In real life, we get really scared and run away."
—ANONYMOUS

• **Curate Your Profile.** Regardless of the platform, your social media account often serves as your first point of contact with prospects. Update your profile with an accurate headshot, details, and contact information. Consider what message your profile is sending, and be consistent across all your accounts: Twitter, Facebook, Instagram, etc.

• **Keep Separate Your Business and Personal Accounts.** Maintain a church-and-state divide in your use of social media. Keep your private dialogues private, and, likewise, don't let your business chatter or commentary bleed into your personal areas. Don't share your personal account with your business contacts until a significant personal relationship has been established.

• **Think Twice.** *Before* posting. Don't respond emotionally or negatively, or engage with controversial topics. Stay away from trolling and angry commentary. Also, think before you tag another person or company in a post. *Always* think again when you have created a message of any kind, and review it carefully before clicking the "Send" button. As Germany Kent said, "There is too much negativity in the world. Do your best to make sure you aren't contributing to it." Remember, whatever you write can be posted somewhere else with your name attached.

• **Be Consistent.** Consistency of topic, message, imagery, and style is important. What's posted on social media is part of your brand

and your mythology. You want people to have specific expectations when they look at your company's account. Social media is an important marketing and PR opportunity for you—so do it right.

- **Be Courteous and Generous.** Kindness, humor, and generosity of spirit will win you followers and connections. Share and re-post good content from your clients, and even from competitors, to build good will. Offer assistance where it's applicable—the world is watching. Build that generous profile and live up to it. Giving is better than getting. If you give people a reason to support you, they will.

- **Proofread.** We're all guilty of typos. But if your messaging includes frequent grammatical errors and mistakes, it will look unprofessional and amateurish, and you will lose followers. An app like Grammarly.com is a great tool for minimizing typos and poor English usage, and can be synced to check your writing on Twitter and LinkedIn.

- **Use Visuals:** Powerful images pull people into your digital content. Poor graphics, by contrast, almost ensure that people will not click in. Invest in high-quality images, and always credit the author/designer/photographer when you post them.

- **Stay Connected and Informed**. Social media is the new news. Use it to stay on top of what your current and potential clients are doing, and be aware of conversations and controversies, industry news, and gossip in your sector: technology, energy, retail, media, financial services, transportation, government, whatever.

- **Stay in Your Lane.** Focus on the best medium for your goals. You cannot have a massive campaign on all the platforms. Pick one or two, and post content that's appropriate for them. Consider your target audience, their demographics, and where they spend their social media time.

• **Provide Value.** Use social media to provide free content: business tips, infographics, instructional videos. By becoming a source of high-quality content, you can often increase your followers, subscribers, and website traffic, and possibly gain new customers more easily than through a hard sell of a product.

Social Media: Don't Try This

"For every action, there is an equal and opposite reaction, plus a social media overreaction."

—ANONYMOUS

• **Don't Be an Idiot.** Don't be that half-naked dude with a bottle of Jägermeister on your head, dancing to the Red Hot Chili Peppers with your best friend's half-naked spouse—and then post a video of it (or let your friends post it). That dude thinks he's killing it, but really he's just killing his job or prospect-hunting chances. Keep in mind that firms do perform online background checks before hiring someone (which sometimes means that job-seekers need to hire someone to scrub their social media footprint).

• **Don't Post Just to Post.** If you pummel your followers with content, you're going to lose your audience. If your material is boring or redundant, then you become boring and redundant. Many people are guilty of over-posting. Be aware that your content can become detritus that nobody looks at. Instead of blather, focus on providing useful content, and make sure it's well put together before posting. Be targeted, and make sure you're not sending the wrong message to the wrong people. Don't overstay your welcome.

• **Don't Move Too Quickly into Sales Mode.** This happens to me almost every day because of the title in my profile and the number of followers I have. People make a connection with me on LinkedIn, then immediately pitch me something or hit me with a cold sales email: "Hi Ed, I was thinking you might want to look at our Egyptian hieroglyphics services because we're really good at them." Wow, you really spent a lot of time looking at my company and what we do. The kiss of death is coming in too early on social media and asking for a connection or a meeting. I will usually shut out anyone who does this and delete the connection. So: don't stalk people, and don't move too fast without at least doing due diligence. Make a polite segue to your business or sales mode after some time has passed.

• **Don't Sound Whiny.** Begging for business or money is not a good look. Ever.

• **Don't Post Spam.** Don't retweet and like and forward again and again. This just fills up your followers' newsfeeds with noise, noise, and more noise—which then leads to your being blocked or tuned out. While you're at it, don't #Overuse #Hashtags either. A little goes a long way.

• **NEVER USE ALL CAPS.** This is viewed by some (like me) as yelling. Yelling never works. (Never use all caps in your emails or texts either.) "WHAT THE HELL ARE YOU TALKING ABOUT??!" you say. Buh-bye.

• **Don't Get Hung Up on Statistics.** It's easy to go down the rabbit hole of worry about how many followers you have or how many followers have retweeted your post or liked your photo. Don't obsess over the numbers. Followers and traffic will come if you send thoughtful, high-quality messages and maintain brand consistency.

• **Don't Forget the Personal Touch.** Perhaps the biggest secret lesson in all of this? As the spread and impact of social media rises, there's even more novelty—and power—in a face-to-face sales call, a coffee meeting, a dinner, or a handwritten note.

CHAPTER 16

MEALS, ENTERTAINMENT, AND EVENTS

EDibles: An Old-Fashioned Guy

"It is very vulgar to talk about one's business. Only people like
stockbrokers do that, and then merely at dinner parties."

—OSCAR WILDE

As mentioned earlier in the book, my mother was the inspiration
for good manners and etiquette becoming my business credo. Anne
Baldry—my name for her was "Momski"—had very old-school
parents, with ties to Her Majesty's Royal Navy, New Zealand, and
mining in Colorado. She had a gregarious nature, a warm sense of
humor, and impeccable manners.

My father, Richard Baldry, served in the military and on the
police force before becoming a stockbroker. He treated people with great respect and was well-respected in return. He was
well-read, spoke, I think, six different languages conversationally
(Spanish, German, Italian, French, Mandarin, and Cantonese, on top
of English), and was also a very funny guy.

My parents met at the 1960 Winter Olympics in Squaw Valley,
California. They laughed a lot, had plenty of friends and fun, and
threw great parties. My father passed away when I was thirty. My
mom passed away a few years ago. The similarity of their personalities—charming, exceedingly polite, and terrifically funny—is probably what drew them together.

I inherited these traits from my parents, and, as a result, I love meeting new people. I love taking folks out for drinks or dinner, hosting parties, and organizing events. I'm meticulous about caring for my guests. I hold doors open for people in public, and yes, even in this day and age, for a female guest I'll pull out the chair when she sits down and stand up when she gets up. I'm not putting on a performance—that is how I was raised to express courtesy and polite manners. These gestures were non-negotiable in my mother's book. (She was famous for subtly jabbing me in the elbow with her fork if I forgot to stand up.) So I suppose these social graces are not so much for my guests' benefit as tributes to Momski.

Even at an event where I'm hosting fifteen or twenty business associates for dinner, I try to address each guest personally. I circulate through the room, switching my position throughout the night to make sure I have a casual conversation with each group of people, and I always try to find something real to talk about.

I guess I'm old-fashioned. But I love making people feel at home. I want to put a smile on people's faces and ensure that they're happy to have met me and have enjoyed the event I've arranged for them. And people, in turn, love to be treated well—and have someone else pick up the tab at the end of the night.

Meals, Entertainment, and Events: The Core Principle

"'Sales Through the Stomach' means ingratiating yourself
to the prospect through fine dining and thoughtful gifts
that really suit their taste."
—TOM NEWTON, CO-FOUNDER AND MANAGING DIRECTOR, ICD

Under any sales team's entertainment umbrella are meals, drinks, and other entertainment events. An event that you specially arrange for someone is an excellent way to attract clients and prospects to your business. Such gestures serve as ways both to thank existing clients and to give prospects a view of your company's culture and success. Sharing good food and drink or a laugh at a comedy show is not just good hospitality; it's a way to wield the power of good manners and etiquette in your business and sales relationships.

Consider these tips and techniques as additional weapons in your "polite and professional communications" arsenal. Many of the ideas in this chapter elaborate on the "killing with kindness" and "wining and dining" advice that I discussed in **Chapter 9: Maintaining Relationships**. Here we're going to drill down a little further. This chapter provides the soup to nuts and nuts and bolts of pulling off the perfect invitation to a lunch or dinner, arranging an outing to a show or sports game, and excelling in those situations where you want to make a good impression and be a good host—until the final "Don't Stop Believin'" karaoke duet has been sung and the last drink has been drained. (For advice on how to host business events like conferences, group meetings, and "road shows," see the **Appendix: A Planning Guide for Business, Sales, and Industry Events**.)

Remember this adage of mine: "Your very first meeting should always be in their office. Every meeting thereafter should involve a fork, a knife, or a glass." Here's the thing: while meeting a client for the first time can be anxiety-provoking, going out to dinner with them, hosting a post-conference shindig for prospects, or taking them to a sporting event or a night on the town can be even more worrisome. There are so many details to keep track of once you get out of the office. You don't want to choose the wrong restaurant, like a paleo steak house for a vegetarian client. You may be trying to impress a guest with your hospitality, and you don't want them to feel that you don't have a clue what you're doing.

No worries. I have some experience with these matters, and I'm happy to show you the way.

A Little Due Diligence. The first step is figuring out what sort of meal, event, or entertainment your prospect or client might enjoy. This should involve some subtle (or not so subtle) sleuthing, or due diligence, to ascertain your client's interests, hobbies, and food preferences—what their idea of fun might be. Here are some ways to get this information:

• Ask around: you might hear second-hand that a business associate loves to play golf, or is a fan of comedy or a particular type of music, or loves a good steak and a glass of wine.

• Ask outright: "We'd love to do something special to show our appreciation, Ms. Shalhoub. What do you and your team like to do for fun?" Or "What's the best corporate event or entertainment you've ever attended?"

• Reach out to contacts who live in your target area to see if they have recommendations or ideas.

• Keep an eye on your guest's local events listings to see what new restaurants have opened, or what bands or shows are coming to that city. Think about (or ask) what kind of entertainment they enjoy.

• Look at the reviews of restaurants, bars, and other venues on Yelp and/or TripAdvisor.

• Know your audience, and match your prospect's personality with the vibe you're trying to create—casual or formal, fun or serious, outrageous or business-only. Are they formal and uptight at all times, or do they play foosball and drink beer in the office on Friday afternoons?

Understand the Rules of Engagement. Does your idea of fun equal fun for them? Understand your client's interests, how they operate, and their level of comfort with the entertainment you're planning. If you offer two seats to the Grammys or the Super Bowl, will that be viewed as cool or as inappropriate payola? Maybe lunch at Chili's is more their speed. For example, some companies won't accept any gift or entertainment valued at more than $50. If you call on Walmart in Bentonville, Arkansas, you'll be having lunch in their cafeteria, and they'll be paying for you. To be compliant and respectful, always ask about a company's entertainment policy.

Who to Invite? Be sure to include appropriate team-members, including the boss if appropriate. One CFO might say, "You know, I don't really go to these things myself. I don't want to make my people nervous in a social setting." Another head honcho might say, "I don't accept that kind of entertainment, but my staff sure does, so please make sure they have a good time." When possible, include your own personal contacts and your clients' colleagues, family, friends, and spouses—this can make clients feel as if they're at a party, not a shakedown.

Meals: Putting the Principle into Play

"I drink to make other people more interesting."
—ERNEST HEMINGWAY

There may be a lot of uncertainty in sales, but one aspect is predictable: in general, people expect to be wined and dined to get your business. To court prospects and keep your business relations viable, you need to become adept at planning food and drink events. You also need to "be the man" or "be the woman" at the bar or restaurant itself and channel your inner "host or hostess with the mostest." Here are some things to keep in mind.

Plan Ahead

"If you fail to plan, you are planning to fail!"
—BENJAMIN FRANKLIN

Whether grabbing a quick cocktail with a client after work or organizing a formal meal for twenty, planning ahead will make the event go more smoothly and remain trouble-free. Try to take care of as many details as possible well in advance of the event. The more organized you are, the less you'll have to worry about on the day itself and the more time you'll have to network and mingle with your clients.

• **What Venue?** Pick an eatery close by that everyone is comfortable with. If you're unfamiliar with the area, ask if your guest has any preferences or suggestions. Consider a restaurant that is economical, neither too casual (like a local watering hole) nor too expensive (like a Michelin 3-star restaurant). Maybe an upscale steak house, possibly followed by a pub or nightclub for after-dinner drinks. If the venue is a bar, be sure to avoid any inappropriate themes (for example, Hooters, strip clubs, or underground cockfighting). Ask if anyone in the party has food restrictions, and make sure the restaurant you choose has options for them.

• **Making Reservations.** Book a table or, better yet, a private function room at an agreed-upon place and time. Confirm the address, the dress code, and, if possible, the location of the table. Don't book or accept a table too close to the restrooms or the kitchen. If the dress code is particular, inform your guests. Call the day before or the day of the event to confirm the reservation.

At the Venue

"This gathering is what I call 'intimate,'
which really means 'Where is everybody?'"
—TIM CONWAY

Ideally, I like to arrive prior to my guests' arrival, to check in with the host and make sure all the final details are set—table size, noise level, daily specials, whatever. I also might arrange for name tags when it's a group of twenty people or more.

• **Get Seated.** I like to think about who's going to sit where. Seat colleagues, clients, and prospects purposefully to allow for appropriate networking. Confirm with your guests that the table offered by the host is adequate and meets their needs. As I've said, I may be an outlier here, but, as a man, I will pull the chair out for a female guest, if I know her well and think she'll appreciate the gesture. I always stand up when a woman stands up, and then I stand again upon her return. Some women find these gestures endearing and Old World; others might be offended or standoffish. Their reaction depends on who they are, and sometimes on their generation. Read the signs and use your judgment.

• **Talk Time.** To begin, make your guests feel comfortable by discussing housekeeping items: coat check, restrooms, timeline, etc. Keep the mood light and fun. Steer the conversation away from shoptalk and toward life events and family. Make sure that any speeches, roasts, and toasts are short and to the point. People will usually want to get back quickly to their food, beverages, and conversation.

• **Minimize Business Talk.** Plan to make the event casual and not too business-y. No sales slideshows during dinner. Leave the laptop at the office. While entertaining guests, keep your mobile off or on silent, and stowed out of sight. Usually I'll have a meeting with my clients during the day to discuss business. If there are additional matters to discuss, depending upon the situation, I might go out to a bar after dinner, one on one or in a smaller group, and bring up the additional business privately at that time. But at a restaurant, I avoid chatting about business.

• **Do Alcohol and Meals Mix?** Try not to encourage or discourage your guests from getting an alcoholic beverage. Similarly, don't feel obligated to get an alcoholic beverage yourself. If you need an excuse, you can always bow out by saying you have a meeting or work to do later that evening.

Especially in sectors like entertainment and finance, alcohol is a big part of the social puzzle. Booze is a social lubricant, but it also involves risks. Dinners are usually safe; it's after dinner that the bad behavior usually happens. If you do drink, don't get hammered and make an ass of yourself, and be sure none of the guests do either. Be on your guard. Enough said.

If you're a guest or a visitor in another country, try to abide by the local cultural norms around drinking. In some countries a drink or two at lunch is acceptable; not so in others. Some hosts may want to test you to see how you handle your liquor. Don't make rookie mistakes, and try to mirror your host. As Phyllis Diller said, "What I don't like about office Christmas parties is looking for a job the next day."

• **Ordering.** Make sure everyone has menus. If there aren't enough, give yours to the nearest guest without one. Tell your guests if it's a set menu or if they can order whatever they like, and relay to the server any food restrictions among the guests. Personally, I like to order a medley of appetizers for all the guests to share. This takes off the pressure to order right away, gets food in their stomachs, and encourages conversation. Ask your server which appetizers are the "best of the house." If you can't decide on how many to order, risk over-ordering and let people take stuff home.

• **Eating.** Don't be Conan the Barbarian. Don't arrive starving. This might be Manners 101, but the basics are worth recapping. Put your napkin on your lap at the beginning of the meal. Never talk with your mouth full or when chewing, and always chew with your mouth closed. Eat slowly, and don't make annoying or disgusting noises. Use the appropriate cutlery at the appropriate time, and pass any communal food (bread, butter, water) to your guests.

Keep in mind the local dining etiquette if you're traveling. You may be expected to eat with your hands in India; to drink a cappuccino before noon in Italy; to avoid eating your bread before your meal in France; or to resist inserting your fork into your mouth in Cambodia. You get the idea.

• **Work It.** This is perhaps the most important element of your event: you. Be in charge. Keep the conversation going. Make sure everyone feels valued, welcome, and important. Do they want more wine? Is the food to everyone's satisfaction? What does everyone want for dessert—deep-fried s'mores, Snickers bites, banana-split ice-cream cake, or pretzel-bottomed Reese's peanut-butter cup cookie pie?

If it's a large group, as the host you need to work the room throughout the evening. Make sure you circulate, talk to each person, and check in with everyone. Be genial and engaging, and control the flow and energy of the event.

• **Take Good Care of and Acknowledge the Service Staff**. This one's easy to execute and shows tons of class. There are few things more painful than watching an intoxicated or self-important person be a jerk to a waiter or waitress. If there's an issue with any aspect of the meal or service, ask about it nicely and discreetly or, even better, step away for a subtle conversation that doesn't make anyone feel awkward.

• **Bend Over Backward to Thank the Staff**. I think a polite acknowledgment toward the end of the event or even a small round of applause is a nice touch. I always try to imagine what I would do if the server were a son or daughter of the client. How would they like you to treat them? Regarding tipping, remember: cheap people suck. Especially if they're using an expense account. Overtip rather than run the risk of undertipping even slightly.

Wrapping Up

> "Hear no evil, speak no evil,
> and you won't be invited to cocktail parties."
> **—OSCAR WILDE**

The meal is over. Don't make it a late night so that no one can work effectively the next day. It's time to go home. Ask your guests if they are all set and wrap up the meal.

• **Getting the Check.** Catch the server's eye and ask for the check. Don't spend an uncomfortable amount of time reviewing it or asking your guest, "Did you know the shrimp scampi you got was $45?" If you're the host and have invited the clients or prospects, you pick up the tab. Period. If you're invited to a dinner, normally you wouldn't pay, but you should definitely offer and go down fighting. Your options:

- "Can I contribute?"
- "May I at least pick up the tip?"
- "How about I pick up some after-dinner drinks or dessert?"

• **Departure.** As folks depart, confirm that everyone has their belongings (coat, blazer, purse, briefcase). When leaving and walking toward the door, let your guests go first, and, when exiting the restaurant, hold the door for them (regardless of gender). Establish whether the evening is over or if you're headed elsewhere for a nightcap.

• **Safe Rides.** When outside the restaurant, and depending upon your location, ask your guests if they need a lift or a cab, and assist them in any way necessary. Make sure that no one drinks and drives. Deceased or incarcerated clients are of no use to you.

Entertainment and Events:
Putting the Principle into Play

"Business is the ultimate sport. In business,
as in sport, the one thing you can control is effort."
—MARK CUBAN

The other kind of hosting that a skilled salesperson should master is pulling off successful non-meal entertainment events. This might mean attending a sports game or an artsy theater performance with your prospect, playing a round of golf with a team of your counterparts, or arranging a special activity like a wine-tasting or a friendly paintball competition. Each of these can be a fun and more casual way to interact with a customer or prospect.

On the planning end, you need to be just as savvy when it comes to planning special entertainment events as you are when planning a meal, in order to show appreciation and good manners. Here are a few points to keep in mind.

Entertainment Ideas. Let's begin with some ideas for alternative business events. Hopefully some of these will jibe with your clients' tastes, based on your previous due diligence.

• **Concerts.** Rock, rap, jazz, folk, classical—whatever will suit your client best. Consider meeting briefly before the concert for a quick drink or bite to eat (or happy hour) and distribute their tickets. Then cut them loose to enjoy themselves. Remember, no one wants their hand held at a show.

• **Theater.** Serious drama or musical theater? See what plays and touring shows are in the area. As with any performance, all communication should take place beforehand, during intermission, or after the event, since it's not considerate to talk during a performance. A quick drink or dessert afterward at a local venue near the theater may be appropriate.

• **Sporting Events.** As with other "crowd" events, it's a good idea to gather somewhere prior to the game, near the stadium or venue, to check in and give out the tickets before your guests watch the action from the third-base line or the fifty-yard line.

If your budget allows, or your company has the perk, a skybox lends itself to business talk. Just remember to keep quiet for the most part and let your guests enjoy the game. Do give significant thought to where you seat each guest; I suggest devising a seating chart to maximize client fun, as well as to confirm that prospects are seated near other guests who will speak positively of your company.

- **Comedy Shows.** Attending these events, usually in clubs and bars, always ensures a great time and makes a strong impression, because sharing a laugh is a powerful way to bond with someone else—as long as you have a good idea of your guest's taste in "funny."

- **Wine-Tastings**. Adding a brief wine-tasting as a feature prior to a dinner or other event, or even offering one as the main event, is becoming a popular idea. Some restaurants have wine cellars, which makes for an impressive setting. Think about hiring a knowledgeable, professional wine expert or sommelier. Wine-tastings provide an easy forum for successful networking.

- **Interactive, Participatory, and Offbeat Events.** If your clients seem open to more unusual kinds of entertainment, consider a dance performance, a visit to an art museum (with fancy cocktails), or a themed event like a Hawaiian-style luau, a pig roast, or other party ('80s theme, anyone?). You might even suggest a group activity that requires guest participation, like karaoke, a lip-synching contest, an escape room, a video-game arcade, a ropes course, a mini-golf tournament, a driving range (or a golf center like Topgolf), a bowling alley, an amusement park, or a cooking class. Be creative, based on what you know about your clients and what you think would rock their world.

Planning Entertainment and Events. Both conventional entertainment and alternative events can involve more moving parts than organizing a restaurant outing.

With sporting, concert, and theater events, contracts and negotiations do come into play, and usually advance payment is required. Work with the stadium or venue's sales executive or liaison. To get the best seats, you may need to use a ticket exchange and resale company such as Live Nation, Vivid Seats, StubHub, or Ticketmaster. Wine-tastings and other specialty events may involve negotiating an agreement of some sort. Sometimes travel arrangements, space rentals, communication with vendors, and coordination with a venue's event-planner are also necessary.

Being the Host. As always, pay attention to your own hosting duties. Just as with a meal, your goal at these events is not only to have fun but to see your clients or prospects in a new light. You want to create a casual environment in which networking is easy and encouraged, in the hope of establishing, or earning, new clients. Seat colleagues, clients, and prospects purposefully, to allow for appropriate networking. And don't forget to have your clients invite their spouses, families, and friends, depending on the type of event.

Bottom line: even if you're running your butt off and never have time to sit down, make the event look easy and seamless to the attendees. When a swan glides gracefully across a pond, its feet are kicking wildly below the surface. That's part of the artistry of hosting: making it look effortless.

Pandemic Protocols: Meals, Entertainment, and Events in the Age of the Coronavirus

"All the world's a stage, and most of us are desperately unrehearsed."
—Seán O'Casey

The coronavirus pandemic has changed our ideas about business interactions and raised some vexing questions about how to pivot to virtual events. How effective is a sales presentation or a dinner party via Zoom? Will in-person sales conferences with hundreds or thousands of attendees even be possible anymore? What virtual entertainment or events will make your clients and prospects feel appreciated?

Perhaps no virtual events will be as successful as in-person activities. Certainly they won't be the same. But I think it's still worth organizing virtual events for your business associates. Salespeople need to adapt and be creative to make their clients feel special, so that they'll tune in and connect despite the distance.

Even without a fancy meal or ball game to offer your guests, creating a warm bubble of good will with a prospect is still possible. Some virtual events can be useful for blowing off steam and offering the chance for casual chat. Other events can be welcome opportunities for socializing or even learning, and can become decent substitutes for in-person networking.

The key is to keep up your business-engagement efforts. Here are some clever and creative ideas for virtual and socially distanced events that will show your appreciation of your clients, as well as their spouses, families, and circles of friends.

• **Online Wine-Tastings.** Send affordable wines that a normal human can buy, $15-20 a bottle. Hire a sommelier to explain (via

207

Zoom or an equivalent app) each wine and the process of picking good wines, while you all enjoy the tasting together, virtually.

• **Meal Deliveries.** Arrange for socially distanced in-person dinner events, or other smaller outdoor gatherings. Or plan a virtual client dinner and arrange to have a local restaurant deliver the food to their house, your treat. For clients who all live in a single area, hire an event producer to arrange for food from a single restaurant, with custom decorations.

• **Drinks.** Offer a virtual happy hour or cocktail/mocktail hour. Pair it with a custom video feed of performers and concerts. Or bring in a mixologist and have participants learn how to make a signature drink for themselves.

• **Professional Development.** Host free virtual co-working and networking events, webinars on useful topics related to the prospects' jobs or business sector, and other informative content.

• **Competitions and Fun.** Put together friendly remote competitions, such as online games, industry-related trivia, dance-off battles (under the age of thirty only, please), or karaoke parties.

• **The Personal Touch.** Send your clients thoughtful personalized information, resources, and other content. For example, if your clients' kids—or the clients themselves—are really into Lego, K-pop, Disney princesses, cooking shows, or some other pop-culture trend, scour the internet and position yourself as a source of information on that topic. Show that you listened to them and remembered their interests.

- **Charity Events.** As an incentive for participation in any of these events, offer to donate money to your clients' favorite charities—better yet, how about a pandemic relief organization?—in honor of any attendee.

- **In the Mail.** One thing that the pandemic reinforces is the value of physical gifts. Send a box of the client's favorite goodies, and accompany it with a classy handwritten note.

CHAPTER 17

HANDWRITTEN NOTES

EDibles: A Letter Is Like a Gift Just for You

"To write is human, to receive a letter divine!"
—SUSAN LENDROTH

I'm reminded of a time early in my career when I made a sales call at UPS. I met with a young professional who worked in treasury technology for the company. After I met with him, I sent a handwritten note to thank him for taking the time to see me. My sense was that members of his generation, digital natives, didn't send or receive many notes. I believe it may have been the first one he ever got, because he pinned up my note in his cubicle, and it was still there when I visited him months later. When he left UPS to go to another firm, he took my note with him. Clearly, it had made an impression. I had built a bridge, a pathway to this guy. To him, my note was almost magical. It turns out that people are starved for personalized touches like this. And they'll hang onto them.

Here's another example. Recently a former colleague sent me a picture of a handwritten note and my business card, which I had sent to him back when I worked for Scudder Kemper Mutual Funds (now owned by Zurich Insurance). That puts the Wayback Machine to 1996. In other words, be forewarned: some people will save what you scribble! I certainly do, especially the impactful letters. If somebody has taken the time to write me a thoughtful message, I can't part with it or toss their handmade, personalized letter into the trash and move on.

The art of the handwritten note harkens back to a different time— when people primarily communicated by hand instead of by keyboard, when folks used fancy ink pens and wrote on fancy linen stationery, perhaps even with the sender's name embossed at the top.

I don't know if a handwritten note ever sealed a deal for me. But countless people have told me that I'm the only person who has ever written them a handwritten note after a meeting or a dinner. To me, feedback like this is a green light to send more and do more, to maintain the connection. That's the whole point of paying attention to these tiny details.

As I discussed in **Chapter 6: Greetings**, handwritten notes are also another way of asking permission, in the form of an expression of appreciation. Neither of these purposes can be accomplished with the click of a button. With a note, you're writing down your thoughts in a personal, handmade way. You're communicating your thanks to an individual, in your own voice. When you do so sincerely, they'll remember these small but intimate gestures—and remember you too, when you connect again.

Handwritten Notes: The Core Principle

"What a lot we lost when we stopped writing letters.
You can't reread a phone call."
—LIZ CARPENTER

We know with a high degree of likelihood that nine out of ten people are not going to take the time to write a handwritten note. Most people will send an email. The advantage of sending a handwritten note is that people love getting mail, especially a proper letter (as long as it's not a bill or junk mail). Even better than mail, people like getting packages. Why? Because people love presents. Consider your letter as a gift to its recipient, meant for their eyes only. Everyone enjoys that feeling of anticipation as they wonder what a letter will say.

A handwritten note isn't a "Reply All" communication; it's between two people. The fact that a pen-and-paper note is not broadcast to a million people makes it all the more powerful. There's no "Look at me, look at me, I'm working so hard to be nice." Rather, a letter offers an individual touch, in the same way that a handshake, a smile, or a one-on-one conversation can be intimate.

While an email or a text is the new normal, an expected way to connect, sending a thoughtful handwritten note conveys a different message—that the writer, you, had enough consideration and appreciation of the person you're communicating with to slow down in your busy world, stop what you were doing, and reach out to them in a customized, unique way. Look at these gestures as opportunities to separate yourself from the pack. In doing so, you can make a powerful impression and differentiate yourself in a time when people aren't differentiating themselves as much anymore. As you stand out, look for a signal—permission—from the contact to enhance your relationship, without ever soliciting anything.

Handwritten Notes: Putting the Principle into Play

"Be thankful for what you have; you'll end up having more.
If you concentrate on what you don't have, you will never,
ever have enough."
—OPRAH WINFREY

You might think that writing a letter is arcane, rare, a dying art form. To write something down on paper, then fold the sheet carefully, stuff it in an envelope, make sure the address is correct and handwrite it, put a stamp on the envelope, and send it through a slow, antiquated mailing system—this process seems absurd. But when the letter reaches the intended party a couple of days later, the effect is vastly different from a text saying, "hey jane great talking to you today see you tomorrow at 1 doug." It's so much more powerful when you've got *real* mail.

The recipient of a handwritten thank you note who feels underappreciated at work will be impressed that you took the time to express your gratitude in this way—that your meeting with them was important enough for you to spend time expressing your thoughts about it. And they'll feel that same genuine appreciation and thoughtfulness when you contact them next. You'll remain at the top of their memory.

Embracing the practice of handwritten notes can take you to the next level of success and help you make an even bigger difference in the lives of people you care about. It's way more impressive than having a dozen LinkedIn recommendations or endorsements.

If it's been a while since you last put pen to paper, here are some tips to make sure your handwritten note has the right impact:

Handwritten Notes Are Good for the Writer Too. Although the reason to write a thank you note is to express your gratitude for something another person has done, the practice benefits you too.

Think of the habit of letter-writing as extreme "mono-tasking," or mindfulness in action. While it's possible to write a thank you email while checking your texts, seeing how many likes your latest Facebook post has gotten, and placing an order on Amazon, you can't do all that when writing a handwritten note. You're forced to concentrate on this one task for a reasonable period. That is the essence of mindfulness: focus or presence. The time and effort that it takes to write the message is a good exercise for the person who's writing it. Call it free therapy to reflect, ponder, slow down. You may not have the time or inclination to meditate, but if you regularly write thank you notes by hand, you will indeed be engaging in this practice.

Letter-writing is the first thing I do in the morning. Number one on my agenda for the day is "Get my thank you notes out." I write them so that I can put them in the mail by the end of the day. And I don't write them in the evening when I'm tired; I write them first thing in the morning, when I have an abundance of energy and enthusiasm.

Get High-Quality Materials. Your words matter most, but so does your presentation. Sure, you can write a message with a disposable ballpoint pen that you grabbed when you donated blood last week, and scribble it on a piece of loose-leaf paper torn out of a spiral-bound notebook. But consider the subtext. Using lousy paper and a crappy pen says, "I took as little time as possible to do this and don't care enough to send you something special." This is the time to splurge. High-quality stationery jumps out. Copier paper and plain white envelopes don't. I order top-quality, personalized notes with matching envelopes. My letterhead includes my name, title, logo, and contact info. I get my stationary from Crane's, but there are other fine companies that make high-quality thank you notes.

I'm also a fan of what I call the "buck slip," a three-by-five card (made of true cardstock) that has my company logo and my personal information (email, phone) printed on it. It's like a giant business card. I like these cards for three reasons. (1) Each one provides a small amount of real estate on which I can fire off a short handwritten note. (2) It's easy to fill up the whole card (versus a larger note, which can leave a lot of blank space). (3) It's another surface on that person's desk or in a drawer where they can find your info, as well as your personalized note.

As for pens, the same advice goes. If you're not an accustomed writer like I am, this directive might seem unusual. What the heck does it matter what you use to write the note with? Well, it matters. A cheap pen can leave smears and little blobs of ink. You want your note to come across as a special piece of correspondence, so spring for a decent pen. Good pens feel and look cool in your hand, and glide across the page. Cross, Lamy, and Parker make good ones for under twenty bucks. I usually write with a pen from Tiffany & Co. or Montblanc. Find your favorite and get a couple extra. And while you're at it, buy a few ink refills so that your pen will be ready when you are.

Whom to Write Notes To. The most important recipient of your personalized note is the person whose office you visited to make a sales presentation, or whatever the occasion. That's the first base to cover. But every person you've met at a meeting should get a note from you. If you were fortunate enough to meet with five people, that means the company is seriously considering your product. Five people chose to leave their desks to listen to you. You're in a pretty good spot, so thank them for their time.

Your handwritten note is also another way of assigning them power. If the recipient is the lowest person on the totem pole, if you send a thank you note addressed to "you and your team," that empowers them.

When and How Often to Write Notes. The trick with handwritten notes is—how often? At which points of contact? When is an email sufficient and not a letter? What determines which response at what level? You want to send the right message at the right time. Don't send a million postcards and love letters via the USPS before you've even met the contact in person. You don't want to appear freaky or inappropriate.

Typically there are three times to send a note: once at the beginning, once in the middle, and once toward the end of a relationship or business transaction.

• **The First Note.** You should send this note shortly after your first face-to-face meeting. The gesture sets the tone for your level of conduct and appreciation. Regardless of how well or poorly the meeting went—even if you feel you bombed—send a thank you note. And send it before you've closed the deal. Reach out and thank the person for the opportunity to meet and speak with them, and/or the opportunity to present what you presented to them, regardless of the outcome.

• **The Second Note.** This might come at the end of your first successful transaction, or after the second time you've connected with them in a meaningful way. Maybe you saw them again at a conference, or had lunch together, or gave them a demo of your product. A meeting with an entire team is another occasion for a note; by then, it's likely that someone has stuck their neck out for you or raised their hand to say, "I'm bringing this guy forward." So thank them again for all they've done, for giving you consideration, for the sale, for the introduction to another person, for the privilege of meeting the team, or for the opportunity to give a demo. Restate your pleasure in meeting them.

• **The Third Note.** This might come when they're making the final decision of whether or not to work with you or take the next step, and you're waiting with baited breath for their reply. "Thank you again for your time and consideration. Please be assured that we are at your service and appreciate your business immensely."

Throughout the process, you want to stay in control.

A final caveat: sometimes I have what I call a "microwave meeting" with somebody at a conference—two minutes long. I get their business card. If the conversation seems promising, I'll write on the back of that business card, "TQ note" (short for "thank you note"). Back home after the conference, I might have fifty cards but, realistically, only half a dozen keepers or contacts worth pursuing. Using buck slips, I'll dash off a quick note to each of these six people: "I want to thank you for stopping by our booth. It was a pleasure to speak with you. I hope our paths cross again. Ed." This isn't jumping down their throat; it's just an expression of "Real nice to meet you, enjoyed the conversation, hope to see you again." I'm certain that very few other conference attendees, if any, do that.

What to Say and How to Say It. This is the most important part of this strategy: what you actually write, the message. But here's the thing about putting pen to paper. That fancy piece of stationery is almost like canvas. You want to make the words count. You might find yourself being more careful, thoughtful, lofty. Or you might feel you've got some verve, or you're a little poetic in your word choice. You're not writing a love letter, but you do want the prose to sing a bit, and be slightly more rhetorical or formal than a text message or email, and a tad more deferential, in a thankful and humble way. Keep that in mind.

Above all, brevity is the soul of wit. The more economical you can make your sincere message, the better it will be received.

In your note, appeal to the person's ego. Mention something specific the person has done and how this has benefited you. Suppose you're a meeting planner. Which of the following notes would you rather receive from a speaker you just hired?

1. *Thank you for your business. I look forward to working with you again soon.*

2. *Thank you for inviting me to speak at the annual conference. I really appreciate your attention to detail, how promptly you responded to my questions over the past several months, and how gracious you were throughout.*

Compliments *do* work. A few lines will do. You don't need to write *War and Peace.*

Here are some examples:

1) *Hello Ms. Brown,*

Thank you for your business. I look forward to working with you again soon.

All the best, Ed

Or: *All the best, EPB*

2) *Hello Ms. Brown,*

Just a brief note to thank you again for your time yesterday. It was a pleasure to meet with you. We are grateful for the opportunity you have afforded us.

We will not let you down.

Or: *We look forward to working with you on this project.*

Or: *We remain at your service if you have any further questions or concerns.*

3) One of my favorite lines to use is this: *We look forward to earning your business.*

That puts the recipient in control and lets them know you're going to work for this deal.

4) When I send a note to more than one person from the same meeting or event, I'll usually say something like: *It was a pleasure to meet with you and your team.*

Or: *Your team is a very impressive group of people.*

Or: *You have assembled a world-class team.*

This message says, "Thank you for the access to your company, to your team, to your people." Once again, compliments work.

While people don't usually share the notes with each other, I'll still try to change at least one line in each note, to make sure I don't repeat myself. To the first person, I might say: *Thanks for the opportunity.*

To the next: *We won't let you down.*

To another: *Looking forward to seeing you again.*

I'll say essentially the same thing to everyone but use a slightly different close for each one, in case they do compare notes (pardon the pun).

5) If a client has brought along a family-member to an event, I'll say: *Thanks for attending the ball game last night. I enjoyed getting to know your husband between innings.*

Or: *I really appreciate your coming out to dinner and bringing your wife along on your personal time.*

Acknowledge that the out-of-office event meant they were spending extra time after work hours with you.

How and When to Mail It. As a general rule, I try to send my handwritten notes within twenty-four hours of the meeting or point of contact with my client or prospect. If you're a Johnny or Janey on the Spot, you can write your notes on the airplane or train home. Writing, "Thank you for your time yesterday," shows that you wrote to them the following day. Even better to write, "Thank you for your time today," and drop the envelope in the mail so that it's postmarked the same day.

If you have an opportunity to mail the note yourself, here are a couple tricks that can make an impression. One is to mail it from the city the recipient is in; you write the note at a coffee shop after the meeting and put it in the mailbox next to their office or at the airport. That says you were so inspired by the meeting that you couldn't wait to tell them. Or mail it from the road. If you met them in Detroit and your home base is in Wichita, mail the note from Kalamazoo, so that your client knows you wrote the note in the hotel and put it in the mail the next day.

If you're traveling abroad, another classy move is to mail the note while you're overseas. Sending a letter from the UK, Germany, or Thailand to the States, or vice versa, is a great move because some people get a kick out of funky postmarks and stamps. Countless people over the years have told me, "I got your note from Switzerland." These are opportunities to make your notes that much more impactful or impressive.

Proofread. This perhaps goes without saying, but make sure you've gone over your note to check for mistakes. Pay attention to your grammar, spelling, and punctuation. Get the name of the recipient right! You might draft it first in a word processor to work the details out. Perhaps have someone you trust give it an edit to make sure there are no run-ons or other errors. Nothing is more embarrassing than writing a letter and having that thoughtful gesture fall flat.

EPILOGUE

An epilogue is usually included in a book to wrap up any loose ends from the plot or project into the future a "what happens next" for the tale, indicating the ultimate fates of the characters. In classical and Elizabethan theater, an actor would often speak directly to the audience and offer some final words, passing judgment on the action or offering a moral.

I'm pretty sure you don't want that. But I do want to leave you with a few thoughts, hopes, and wishes for the future.

First, to you, my reader, consider this my humble thank you note. I'm sorry I can't handwrite, personalize, and send a note to each and every one of you. But I do appreciate your time, attention, and consideration. And I hope this book has transformed you in some way (hopefully for good and not for evil).

As my hero Robin Williams once said, "You're only given a little spark of madness. You mustn't lose it." It takes a little madness to succeed in business and sales. You have to push, pitch, and persist. Perhaps only the most driven, or the craziest, can survive. As I said at the beginning of this book, I see "please" as the starting gun of polite and professional communications. This final "thank you" need not be the end. I hope you will keep growing and learning as a salesperson, a businessperson, and a human being.

Now, here's my prediction for the future. As I gaze into my crystal ball, I see a time when, some day not so distant from now, we will have changed. As a culture and society, we will reconnect with our traditions of manners and etiquette. I see a time when we'll find those values and traditions and express them anew, in profound ways, once more.

And with that perhaps naive vision, I wish you all the best, and hope our paths cross again soon.

APPENDIX

A Planning Guide for Business, Sales, and Industry Events, by Nancy G. Duggan, Co-Founder, COO, EPBComms, LLC

Hosting Conferences, Group Meetings, and "Road Shows"

The ultimate way to show appreciation and gratitude for your clients and prospects—and to work all the magic of transferring enthusiasm, maintaining relationships, and showing fine business manners and etiquette—is to host your own business event.

This event might be staged at an existing conference as a "road show," or you might organize your own "summit" for your pool of contacts—a big meeting, retreat, or mini-conference for your most trusted partners and clients and for promising potential customers.

These events differ in complexity from the ones we covered in **Chapter 16: Meals, Entertainment, and Events**. There's much more to arrange than just food and drink and a trip to the ballpark, and the scale usually requires a team of people to execute every detail.

In the past, at ICD, my colleagues and I hosted a range of events in most of our major markets: San Francisco, Los Angeles, Chicago, Atlanta, New York City, Boston, and London. These events varied in length from one day to two or three days. They usually focused on either showing appreciation to our clients or using presentations and small breakout sessions to educate them on new products, technology, and upgrades. The size and duration of the events were usually tied to the number of clients or prospects we were trying to entertain or educate. Of course, we arranged for plenty of fun and games in and around all the business.

Here's what you need to consider when putting on one of these more complex events:

Think About Content. The events my team organized were intended, first and foremost, to promote the company. The content, or "program," might include:

• Sales/PowerPoint presentations, training sessions, and other professional-development opportunities. I suggest keeping the business and sales sessions to a minimum.

• Brief speeches by yourself and other key colleagues.

• Added benefits like motivational speakers or talks by other industry experts.

• Ample chances to break out into smaller groups.

• Networking opportunities for attendees.

• A meal or buffet of light food and beverages, based on your timeline.

• A band or DJ-ed dancing, perhaps followed by an off-site after-event gathering at a fun venue like a jazz club. Or you might arrange for a special luncheon, dinner party, or late-night beverage or snack.

Find the Venue. Do online and referral research for the type of venue you're looking for, and take into consideration the following:

• The city where the event will be held, and what attractions and activities that city offers.

• The number of attendees, and whether a small or large room will be required. If the event will be held at a hotel, usually a conference room of average size will suffice (versus booking an entire ballroom). Nine times out of ten, however, I like to host events at restaurants because the food and beverages at hotels tend to be average, with outrageous prices and fees attached.

• Book all hotel accommodations well in advance, and make sure the hotel is relatively close to the event venue, within walking distance if possible.

• Do a site visit in advance to confirm that the venue will work for your event.

Collaborate with Sponsors. These events can be pricey for a company. One option to offset the cost is to collaborate with your colleagues, partners, or industry leaders to find a sponsor or co-sponsor for the event. In many instances your target audience or clients will be the same for another vendor or complementary product. If you become skilled at planning these events, people will line up to attach their name to them and gain access to your level of entertainment.

The goal: you plan the party, someone else pays for it. Here's how that might work:

• Plan an event with another organization and split the tab. Their attendance will allow for additional monies to offset your budget.

• Plan an event independently and then ask potential sponsors to come aboard for an agreed-upon fee. Sponsors usually provide swag or marketing materials, in return for the exposure when a partner markets the event with their name and branding.

• Think about having your sponsor be a partner organization that you already work with, which can bring an additional component to the event, such as a specialist within your specific industry.

Plan Ahead. Keep in mind that the success of the event is on you, in your role as host, salesperson, and event-planner. Your due diligence and advance planning—at least three to six months prior to the event—will determine its outcome. The more prepared and organized you are, the more successful the event will be.

Coordinate and collaborate with the venue's event-planner(s). Do your due diligence on all aspects of the venue, including contracts, pricing, and policies. This process might include:

• Ensuring the availability of the venue for your preferred times and dates.

• Executing the contract, including all deadlines, pricing, deposits, and deliverables, which you must carefully review. Note: the contract should include arrival and departure times, and some venues may charge for overages.

• Asking if parking is included and if validation is required.

• Writing out directions to the venue, and ensuring that the timeline and flow of the event is agreed-upon and understood.

• Reviewing the floor plan: the room size, the set-up of tables, chairs, linens, and centerpieces, the location of the restrooms, and disability accommodations.

• Going over the menu, inquiring about food preferences and restrictions, and confirming pricing.

• Checking the set-up and availability of all the tech devices that will be used during the presentations: projectors, monitors, laptops, cabling, connections, internet access, microphones, whiteboards, etc. Also determine if an on-site tech team will be available and, if so, what their fees are.

• Discussing and tying down any and all logistics that might affect the success of your event.

• Negotiating. There is always room for negotiation. At the hotel where the team and guests will stay, negotiate the pricing for accommodations if you're also using the hotel's event space. Pit one vendor against the other: "Joe's Steakhouse is only charging $50 per head. Can you meet or beat that?" Most places will want your business and will negotiate in some way.

Checklists: Before, During, and After the Event. Here are check-lists of what to take care of in the weeks and days leading up to your event, the day of the event, and afterward:

Before the Event

• Coordinate with your team and colleagues to prepare for all the presentations, including any content, materials, and digital decks needed for the event.

• Connect well in advance with the presenters and producers to confirm that everyone is on the same page, and to establish proto-cols, timelines, and workflows for the event.

• Communicate and market the details of the event to all the attend-ees and potential attendees. Include event logistics well in advance: who, what, when, where, why, and how. Use social media to create excitement. The more information your attendees have in advance and the more prepared they are, the better the outcome will be.

• Be sure that all the attendees have contact info for you or a repre-sentative of your team, should any problem come up on the day of the event. This will help to avoid last-minute crises.

• The day before the event, call the venue and confirm and recon-firm all of the logistics. Confirm the names and contact info of the staff you'll be working with on the day of the event.

At the Event

• Get to the venue two to three hours before the start time. Even before that, inform the venue event-planner of the time of your arrival.

• Bring everything you'll need with you, and a bunch of stuff you won't think you'll need, including:

> • Contact info for all of the venue's staff-members
>
> • Several copies of the attendee list
>
> • The seating plan/arrangements
>
> • A copy of the contract and all pertinent documents
>
> • Marketing hand-out materials
>
> • Name tags (review and memorize some of the attendees' names and the companies they're affiliated with—this will enable light conversation when you're checking them in)
>
> • Miscellaneous: phone charger, pens, Kleenex, thumb drives, toothpicks, hand sanitizer, Emergen-C, Advil, etc. (you wouldn't believe what guests will ask you for)

• Ensure that all attendees' needs are met, that the content of the meeting is appropriate, and that they can all hear the presentations. Also ensure that they're networking and have the correct quality and quantity of food and beverage. Remember, you're the host, so everything and anything you can do to make sure your guests are comfortable, engaged, and having fun is another way to express good manners and etiquette. Always be polite, and interact with everyone in a hospitable and professional way.

After the Event

• Send a note or email to each of your attendees individually, thanking them for attending.

• Send a note or email to each of the venue's staff-members that you worked with, to thank them for their hard work in making the event a huge success.

WORKS CITED

The majority of the practices, principles, and protocols in *It Begins with Please and Doesn't End with Thank You* originated in the dark recesses of my brain—either from my professional on-the-job experience or from the wisdom and advice I've received (or stolen) from colleagues and mentors. That said, I did find several books, articles, and blog posts useful, informative, and in some cases eye-opening. Often I've directly mentioned studies and research and quoted specific writers. I would be remiss in not mentioning these additional sources:

Balinas, Travis. "Social Media Etiquette for Business Owners: 25 Do's & Don'ts." *Outbound Engine* (February 20, 2020). https://www.outboundengine.com/blog/social-media-etiquette-for-business-25-dos-donts.

Bomey, Nathan. "How Do We Replace the Business Handshake in the COVID-19 Era?" *Charleston Regional Business Journal* (May 20, 2020). https://charlestonbusiness.com/news/human-resources/78553/.

CircleHD. "6 Strategies for Successful Remote Sales During a Pandemic" https://www.circlehd.com/blog/remote-sales-prospecting-coronavirus.

Cuncic, Arlin. "How to Practice Active Listening." *Very Well Mind* (May 25, 2020). https://www.verywellmind.com/what-is-active-listening-3024343.

The Daily Zen Journal. "Transmission of Mind" (November 9, 2009). https://www.dailyzen.com/journal/transmission-of-mind.

Deitch, Joseph. *Elevate: An Essential Guide to Life* (2018).

Durr, Jeff. "Building Exceptional Business-to-Business Relationships." *Gallup.* https://www.gallup.com/analytics/231674/building-exceptional-business-business-relationships.aspx.

Frost, Aja. "How to Text Sales Prospects (and Double Your Conversion Rate)." *HubSpot* (January 21, 2020). https://blog.hubspot.com/sales/text-sales-prospects.

Graeber, David. *Debt: The First 5,000 Years* (2011).

Gurchiek, Kathy. "Coronavirus: Time to Rethink the Handshake." *SHRM* (March 16, 2020). https://www.shrm.org/hr-today/news/hr-news/pages/coronavirus-time-to-rethink-the-handshake.aspx.

Hafner, Christopher. "What Is Qi? (and Other Concepts)." *Taking Charge of Your Health and Well-Being,* University of Minnesota. https://www.takingcharge.csh.umn.edu/explore-healing-practices/traditional-chinese-medicine/what-qi-and-other-concepts.

Harbinger, AJ. "7 Things Everyone Should Know about the Power of Eye Contact." *Business Insider* (May 14, 2015). https://www.businessinsider.com/the-power-of-eye-contact-2015-5.

Hart, Meredith. "Video Conferencing Etiquette: 10 Tips for a Successful Video Conference." *Owl Labs* (March 25, 2020). https://www.owllabs.com/blog/video-conferencing-etiquette.

Harvard Medical School, Division of Sleep Medicine. "Sleep and Mood" (December 15, 2008). http://healthysleep.med.harvard.edu/need-sleep/whats-in-it-for-you/mood.

Hoffman, Claire. "6 Ways Event Planners Can Maintain Client Relationships During the COVID-19 Outbreak." *Biz Bash* (April 7, 2020). https://www.bizbash.com/production-strategy/strategy/article/21126515/6-ways-event-planners-can-maintain-client-relationships-during-the-covid19-outbreak.

Hoffman, Jeff. "Call or Email? 5 Tips to Determine When to Use Which in Sales." *HubSpot* (April 14, 2020). https://blog.hubspot.com/sales/call-or-email-tips-to-determine-when-to-use-which-in-sales.

Illig, Randy. "Put Your Thinking Caps On: How to Sell During the Coronavirus Pandemic." *Forbes* (March 17, 2020). https://www.forbes.com/sites/randyillig/2020/03/17/put-your-thinking-caps-on-how-to-sell-during-the-coronavirus-pandemic.

Jackson, Dominique. "Twitter vs. Instagram: Which Is Best for Your Brand." *Sprout Social* (October 12, 2015). https://sproutsocial.com/insights/twitter-vs-instagram/.

Job Monkey. "How To Shake Hands Professionally" (August 14, 2018). https://www.jobmonkey.com/shake-hands-professionally.

Kats, Rimma. "Virtual Events May Be the Norm Post-Pandemic." *eMarketer* (June 25, 2020). https://www.emarketer.com/content/virtual-events-may-norm-post-pandemic.

Kaye, Jezra. "If You Want to Get Called Back, Leave a Clear Phone Message." *Speak Up for Success.* https://speakupforsuccess.com/phone-message-skills/.

Keough, Ben. "The Best Videoconferencing Service." *The New York Times: Wirecutter* (June 24, 2020). https://www.nytimes.com/wirecutter/reviews/best-video-conferencing-service/.

Kramer, Ariel. "7 Steps to Take When Scrubbing Your Social Media Presence, According to Branding and PR Experts." *Business Insider* (September 27, 2019). https://www.businessinsider.com/scrub-social-media-delete-job-application-2019-9.

Krle, Elena. "How Eye Contact Can Help You Succeed in Business and Life." *The Good Men Project* (March 22, 2019). https://goodmenproject.com/guy-talk/how-eye-contact-can-help-you-succeed-in-business-and-life-cmtt/.

Miller, Claire Cain. "How to Be More Empathetic." *The New York Times: A Year of Living Better* (January 31, 2019). https://www.nytimes.com/guides/year-of-living-better/how-to-be-more-empathetic.

Oaklander, Mandy. "The Coronavirus Killed the Handshake and the Hug. What Will Replace Them?" *Time* (May 27, 2020). https://time.com/5842469/coronavirus-handshake-social-touch/.

Pachter, Barbara. *The Essentials of Business Etiquette: How to Greet, Eat, and Tweet Your Way to Success* (2013).

Patel, Sujan. "Phone Call or Email? How to Choose the Right Sales Outreach Approach." *Entrepreneur* (October 15, 2018). https://www.entrepreneur.com/article/319526.

Popova, Maria. "How We Got 'Please' and 'Thank You.'" *Brain Pickings* (July 25, 2013). https://www.brainpickings.org/2013/07/25/origin-of-please-and-thank-you/.

Ram Dass. "Huang-Po and the Transmission of Mind" https://www.ramdass.org/huang-po-and-the-transmission-of-mind/.

Reedsy. "What is an Epilogue? Definition and Step-by-Step Guide" (January 31, 2020). https://blog.reedsy.com/what-is-an-epilogue/.

Price-Mitchell, Marilyn. "Goal-Setting Is Linked to Higher Achievement." *Psychology Today* (March 14, 2018). https://www.psychologytoday.com/us/blog/the-moment-youth/201803/goal-setting-is-linked-higher-achievement.

Schwarzman, Stephen A. *What It Takes: Lessons in the Pursuit of Excellence* (2019).

Schilling, Dianne. "10 Steps To Effective Listening." *Forbes* (November 9, 2012). https://www.forbes.com/sites/womensmedia/2012/11/09/10-steps-to-effective-listening.

Shebel, Melanie. "Funny Email Signatures & Sign-Offs." *Turbo Future* (July 24, 2020). https://turbofuture.com/internet/Funny-Email-Signatures.

Spector, Nicole. "Smiling Can Trick Your Brain into Happiness—and Boost Your Health." *NBC News* (November 28, 2017). https://www.nbcnews.com/better/health/smiling-can-trick-your-brain-happiness-boost-your-health-ncna822591.

Turkle, Sherry. *Reclaiming Conversation: The Power of Talk in a Digital Age* (2015).

Weir, Kirsten. "The Exercise Effect." *American Psychological Association*, v. 42, n. 11 (November 2011). https://www.apa.org/monitor/2011/12/exercise.

Wong, Kristin. "The Benefits of Talking to Yourself." *The New York Times* (June 8, 2017). https://www.nytimes.com/2017/06/08/smarter-living/benefits-of-talking-to-yourself-self-talk.html.

ACKNOWLEDGMENTS

There are a lot of people to thank!

First and foremost, I would like to acknowledge my beautiful wife, Gwen, and my outstanding sons, Michael and Evan. Without their support over the years, my career would not have been possible. I am forever grateful for their patience and their forgiveness of my selfish behavior.

This book would not have been possible without the remarkable editorial and writing assistance of Ethan Gilsdorf. Thank you, Ethan, for making this book a reality.

Thank you to Doug and Nancy, my former colleagues at ICD and partners at EPBComms, for being so supportive, helping me start the next chapter of my life, and helping to construct this book as well.

Thank you to my sister, Phyllis Harrelson, for being a moral compass and the kindest, most loving example of character on the planet.

Thank you to my former partners and life-long brothers, Tom and Jeff. I simply would not be here today if it were not for you. Thank you both for this journey.

In addition, thank you...

To a few mentors and managers:

Bobby Boemer, for being the best big brother and my comedic guiding star.

Chuck Maguire, for his unrelenting need to coach and teach young people.

Chris Klutch, for access to his acumen. A true Sensei.

Mark Casady, for his leadership and joy.

Mike Harrington, for his guidance, his sense of humor, and the patience of a saint.

Rob Willms, for his friendship and always level guidance.

David Haugh, for his humor, love of life, and appreciation of all people.

Dan O'Toole, for seeing something in the seventeen-year-old version of me. Your impact has been immeasurable.

Michael Campbell, for being the Barry White of the banking world and a terrific friend over twenty-five years.

Jeff Schwartz, for being quite simply the best entrepreneur and business person I have ever seen.

Jane Moran, for sharing her incredible talent and shattering every ceiling put above her.

To all of my clients over the years. There are too many to mention, but a few I must single out:

Connie Linhart, for the opportunity and for hundreds of references provided.

Mark Sahler, for his wisdom, advice, and friendship throughout and beyond my career.

From the TYCO Tree: Kathy Cahill, Marc Rudnick, Bao Tran, Magnus Svensson, and—*in memoriam*—Joe Byrne.

Brett Taylor, for putting ICD on the map in Atlanta.

Conor Maher, for his humor and advice and for putting ICD on the map in the UK and Europe.

ACKNOWLEDGMENTS

Anthony McCreary, Rick Oleck, and Garry Sealock for the opportunity of a lifetime. You and Freddie changed our industry.

To my closest friends on the planet, who have supported me through everything:

Brigham Hausman and Pablos Anastasopoulos: from the very beginning to today, you two always helped the world make sense.

Scott Prosser, Paul Schulte, Todd Weinstein, and Scott Sledge: "All my friends take good care of me"—The Revivalists.

Jon Salamida, for the interview with Lanier that I never made.

David Groom, for your lessons in philanthropy and life. You have become like a brother to me.

Gary Gadsden, for being the best friend and person I have ever known.

Mason Martin, for sticking with me for over twenty years and changing my life.

James Greenway, for your loyalty and all the music, humor, and conversation.

Rob Speer, for being enormously funny and multi-talented: the ultimate sales, fishing, guitar, and tequila aficionado.

Emmanuel Amapakabo (Manu), for being my biggest fan literally and figuratively. You made London a special experience for my whole family.

To my unforgettable colleagues:

Tory Hazard, ICD's all-time most important hire. The best businessman I ever worked with.

Craig Stevens, for your loyalty, professionalism, and trust.

Russ Driver, cherished friend and brother-in-arms.

Luke Newman, bulletproof operational ICD stalwart and the future of Fintech Sales.

Magda Macdonald, my most important and impactful hire in all of my years in London.

Sebastian Ramos, simply the smartest and hardest-working guy in any room.

To those I have omitted, my sincere apologies. Please know that it would require another 200 pages for me to list all the fantastic people who have made my journey possible. To all my friends, fans, and supporters, thank you from the bottom of my heart.
—EPB

ABOUT THE AUTHOR

Edwin P. Baldry is the Co-Founder and CEO of EPBComms, LLC, an international enterprise that connects the worlds of business communications and financial technology. EPBComm's professional-services portfolio offers strategic communications, sales and marketing, business development, entrepreneurs in residence, live-event and media production, and professional speaking featuring topical humor and deep industry insight.

Baldry is a pioneer in the financial technology sector. In 2003, he and his founding partners launched Institutional Cash Distributors (ICD), which transformed liquidity solutions and risk-management practices for corporate treasuries. Baldry propelled ICD to the top of the institutional marketplace, making it the world's largest independent money-market fund portal. It currently services over $200 billion in assets under management. Before his tenure at ICD, Baldry served as director of the Institutional Money Fund business at Deutsche Bank/Scudder.

Prior to his financial career, Baldry worked as a stand-up comedian in San Diego, performing at the Improv and Comedy Store and other Southern California venues. Baldry transitioned to slightly more serious public speaking in the treasury/fintech industries. He is a recognized professional speaker with the NSA (National Speakers Association) and has appeared at AFP, ACT, ATEL, and ICD's international road shows, as both a speaker and a moderator. Baldry and his wife, Gwen, and their two sons reside in Florida.

For more information, visit epbcomms.com or listen to Baldry's podcast, *EdTalks*.

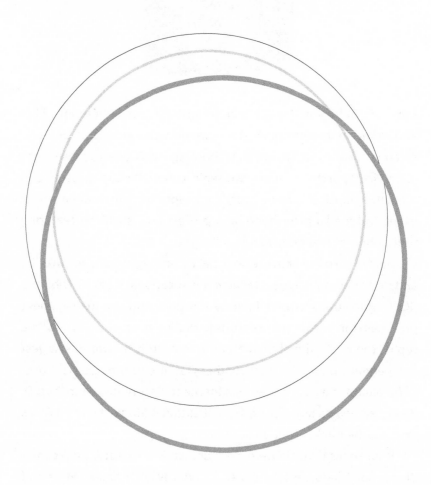